COOKING

FRESH

from the

BAY AREA

The Bay Area's Best Recipes
for Eating Local, Organic Produce
at its Seasonal Best

COOKING
FRESH
from the

BAY AREA

The Bay Area's Best Recipes
for Eating Local, Organic Produce
at its Seasonal Best

Eating Fresh
GUIDES

Foreword by Nell Newman

Introductions by Sibella Kraus & K. Dun Gifford

Compiled & Edited by Fran McManus & Wendy Rickard

*Dedicated
to the
independent
farmers who
are working
to grow a
better world
and
to Ian, Evan,
and Chloe for
providing the
best reasons
for wanting it
to be a
healthier —
and more
delicious —
place to live*

About EATING FRESH^{SM}

Eating Fresh seeks to connect consumers to local agriculture and to demonstrate the taste, health, and community benefits of eating local, seasonal, organic food. Through regional cookbooks and other venues, Eating Fresh works to help build local food systems and to spark a national campaign to transform the way we shop, cook, and think about food.

Eating Fresh^{SM} • 16 Seminary Avenue • Hopewell, NJ 08525
609-466-1700 • www.eatingfresh.com

———————————

Cooking Fresh from the Bay Area

Published by Eating Fresh^{SM} Publications
Copyright ©2000 by Fran McManus and Wendy Rickard
The Growing Danger of Monocropping ©2000 by Peter Jaret

Excerpt from *Sharing the Harvest: A Guide to Community Supported Agriculture* reprinted with permission from Elizabeth Henderson; *8 Simple Steps to the New Green Diet* reprinted with permission from Mothers & Others for a Livable Planet; excerpt from *The Pesticide Question: Environment, Economics and Ethics* reprinted with permission from David Pimentel.

Cover design and illustration: Diana Howard
Cover photograph: Grant Peterson
Recipe editors: Martha Hester Stafford and Gerry Gould
Recipe tester: Joseph George
Proofreader: Paula Plantier

Printed in the United States on recycled paper.

First Edition

ISBN: 0-9673670-0-X
Library of Congress Catalog Card Number: 99-76979

Contents

FOREWORD by Nell Newman vii

PREFACE COOKING FRESH FROM THE BAY AREA ix

ACKNOWLEDGMENTS xi

INTRODUCTIONS

    WHY CHEFS CARE ABOUT SUSTAINABLE AGRICULTURE by K. Dun Gifford xii

    SUPPORTING THE AGRICULTURAL ABUNDANCE OF THE BAY AREA by Sibella Kraus xiii

PART ONE: WINTER

    WINTER CROPS 3

    THE RHYTHM OF WINTER by Paul Muller 5

    BAY AREA FARMS by Tom Haller 6

    FARMERS MARKETS by Gail Feenstra 7

    BUYING LOCAL MAKES GOOD NEIGHBORS by Michael Shuman 8

    WHAT IS COMMUNITY-SUPPORTED AGRICULTURE? by Elizabeth Henderson 10

    COMMUNITIES THAT GROW THEIR OWN MONEY by Tim Cohen-Mitchell 11

    WINTER RECIPES 13

PART TWO: SPRING

    SPRING CROPS 47

    THE FARM LIFE by Denesse Willey 49

    WHAT IS ORGANIC? by Elizabeth Henderson 50

    CAN WE HAVE AN ORGANIC FOOD SYSTEM? by Mark Lipson 51

    GOOD HEALTH STARTS WITH GOOD SOIL by Joel Simmons 52

    8 SIMPLE STEPS TO THE NEW GREEN DIET by Mothers & Others 54

    SPRING RECIPES 57

PART THREE: SUMMER

    SUMMER CROPS 87

    A TASTE OF SUMMER by Stuart Dickson 89

    THE GROWING DANGER OF MONOCROPPING by Peter Jaret 90

    SEEDS: AGRICULTURE'S VANISHING HERITAGE by Hope Shand 94

    EATING WITH CONSCIENCE by Gary L. Valen 95

    UNBLEMISHED FRUITS & VEGETABLES & PESTICIDE USE by David Pimentel 96

    SUMMER RECIPES 97

PART FOUR: FALL

    FALL CROPS 127

    FARMING IN THE FALL by Jim Cochran 129

    SAVING THE LAND THAT FEEDS AMERICA by Bernadine Prince 130

    A FARM WOMAN'S OPINION by Marion Long Bowlan 132

    GETTING LOCALLY GROWN FOODS INTO SUPERMARKETS by Mothers & Others 133

    EAT FRESH, EAT LOCAL by Wendy Rickard 135

    YEAR-ROUND-AVAILABILITY CHART 136

    PRODUCE STORAGE AND PRESERVATION CHART 137

    BUY ORGANIC by Carl Smith 138

    THE NATURAL STEP TO SUSTAINABILITY by Terry Gips 140

    FALL RECIPES 143

RESOURCES CHEFS, AUTHORS, FARMS & FARM PRODUCTS, ORGANIZATIONS, NOTES 170

INDEX 176

I feel lucky to have been raised in an environment that nurtured my idealism. In rural Connecticut my family didn't have a farm, but we did have chickens and a number of old apple trees. Whatever apples I didn't get, the chickens did. In the summer we bought our produce from a local farm stand.

My formative years were spent fishing with my father and learning to cook with my mother using our own eggs and apples as well as produce from the farm stand. Dad and I caught fish and ate them with fresh corn and tomatoes. He really taught me about produce. He taught me the hollow sound of a ripe watermelon and that perfect scent of a sweet cantaloupe. I had a direct connection to my food; I knew where it came from. I grew it and picked it, or I caught it and cleaned it.

Foreword

Then, when I was 11, I had an eye-opening experience. The budding biologist in me was shocked to discover that my favorite animal, the peregrine falcon, was about to go extinct in the United States as a result of exposure to DDT. At the time I had a vague idea of what extinction meant from visiting museums and seeing the animals. But in my young mind it was hard to grasp that this was going to happen in my lifetime. Soon after, to add insult to injury, both the farm stand and the orchard in my home-town disappeared and the first condominium complex was built on that land.

In retrospect, I believe those two events shaped my view of the world, and they continue to influence my life and my business. After getting my degree in human ecology, I became involved with the restora-tion—here in California—of the bald eagle and the peregrine falcon, both of which had been decimated by pesticides and human encroachment. Fortunately, the efforts of individuals and nonprofits managed to reestab-lish populations of bald eagles and peregrine falcons in the United States. And though both are thriving, the long-term effects of new pesticides and herbicides is still unknown.

As I moved from the nonprofit world into the business world, I did so convinced that organic agriculture was the crucial yet missing piece of the puzzle. When I worked in the nonprofit world, I used to joke that I was tired of trying to raise money every year, that I just wanted to give it away like Dad did. I thought if I could do an organic product, I could support organic agriculture. Realistically, I knew the effect would be small, but if we were lucky and we grew, we would be able to increase the acres that are farmed organically—and correspondingly, reduce pesticide use.

I'm happy we've managed to realize some success, but there is still much work to be done. As the family chef and someone who grew up eating from the local farm stand, I've always been partial to the taste and quality of fruits and vegetables picked fresh from the local family farm. The relentless paving over of some of our region's best farmland means more than just losing open space to suburban sprawl. It means losing a connection to our food and to the people who grow it.

The best way to rebuild a connection to food is to know your local farmers and to purchase the products they raise. The chefs, farmers, and individuals you'll meet in this book all have made that connection. Under their guidance, you'll learn the joys of eating local produce at its seasonal peak. You'll discover the simple, elegant philosophy that underlies organic farming. And you'll understand why spending food dollars with local farmers is a wise investment. The impact of each individual purchase may feel insignificant, but the combined effect is profound.

Nell Newman
Aptos, California
September 1999

Food. We need it to survive. It brings us pleasure. It comes with its own set of frustrations: too much makes us fat, not enough makes us frail. It defines us: "I like Chinese food," "I dislike Brussels sprouts," "I'm a vegetarian," "I can't tolerate dairy." It is intricately tied to our bodies, our minds, our sensuality, our social lives, our fears, and our individual and collective consciousness.

Cooking Fresh from the Bay Area

With this in mind, it is no wonder that the food industry is complex, contradictory, and powerful. Everywhere we turn there's information about food, but as consumers we don't generally feel informed. Instead, we are confused by the labels, the reports, the magazine articles, and the endless parade of programs meant to show us how food can make us happy, healthy, thin, sexy, heart strong, alert, and at peace.

What has happened to our relationship with food? To begin, the distance between farm and table has grown endlessly—and needlessly—far, making it difficult, if not impossible, to know where our food is from, how it was raised, and how far it has traveled. And we have become party to a social, economic, and political system that would have us believe it doesn't matter—that as long as food is cheap and abundant, we are well off. Fast foods have dulled our senses and retrained our palates away from what instinctively we crave. Packaged foods take up more shelf and aisle space in our grocery stores than do fresh foods. In short, the past few decades of the food industry have been about cheap ingredients, clever packaging, and promises of great taste, better health, and convenience. And still, we don't feel well, we don't know what to eat, and we have no idea what to buy. We are entwined in a system whose success depends on separating us from the source of our food.

However you slice it, the source of food is a farm. And how that farmer chooses to farm—as well as how far farm products need to travel—says a lot about how the food will taste. Chefs know this, which is why more and more of America's best chefs are going directly to small, local family farms for ingredients. Consumers know this, which is why more and more of us are turning to local farms, farm markets, and natural and organic groceries for everyday ingredients. Support for sustainable and organic agriculture has expanded beyond environmentalists to include food enthusiasts, home cooks, health care providers, and local communities. And that support comes from a desire for the best-tasting, freshest ingredients, grown with little or no chemical pesticides or fertilizers.

As small family farms get paved over to make room for condominiums and office parks, we are beginning to notice the effects. Whether we live in cities, suburbs, or rural America, we're beginning to understand that farming not only contributes to our health and well being; it is also an important part of a community's economy. Farms provide much-needed open space and jobs. Farm owners and workers purchase local goods and services, thereby keeping rural communities vibrant. Local farms make it possible for us to get to know who grows our food, much the same way we know our shopkeepers, tailors, and local restaurateurs.

Cooking Fresh from the Bay Area was not born out of a desire to lose weight, lower cholesterol, or reinvent cooking. It began with the realization of the connection between superior flavor and local farm products. It was born out of the remembrance of what a melon tastes like fresh from the farm. Or a peach. Or a tomato. Or a squash. It began with getting back to what it means for food to be fresh.

We wanted to let the world know what chefs have known for a long time: fresh, locally grown ingredients produced by farmers who believe in sustainable and organic agriculture are superior in both flavor and quality. So we pulled together 20 of the area's most exciting chefs, who gave us their best recipes for cooking with local, seasonal ingredients. But that's only part of the picture. We also pulled together farmers and other experts, who could explain, in simple terms, the environmental, social, and economic benefits of buying, cooking, and eating locally grown, organic foods at their seasonal best.

What we learned—and what this book promotes—is that eating fresh means eating locally, seasonally, and organically. We learned that getting back to the source of our food is not only sensible but also fun and delicious. And while it is difficult to buy nothing but locally grown ingredients, doing so even to a small extent means better-tasting meals and healthier communities.

Get to know your local farmer. Eat fresh. Eat local.

Fran McManus
Wendy Rickard
Hopewell, New Jersey
November 1999

We would like to extend endless thanks and deep gratitude...

...to the chefs and authors who contributed so graciously to this book. Your generosity and enthusiasm helped us define—and realize—our vision.

...to Joe George, Gerry Gould, Diana Howard, Grant Peterson, Paula Plantier, and Martha Hester Stafford. Your individual and collective talents, skills, and expertise challenged us to go further than we imagined possible. We look forward to many future collaborations.

Acknowledgments

...to the late Gary Holleman for his encouragement when this all began.

...to all of you who took the time to share your knowledge, experience, and opinions on marketing, research, and publishing as well as on food and farming. To John Clark, Michael Dimock, Peter Feld, Chet Grycz, Chuck Hassebrook, Mary Hayes, Ellen Hickey, Betsy Lydon, Francis Lynch, Christine Maxwell, Andrew Powning, Tori Ritchie, Laurie Roberge, Bob Scowcroft, Rebecca Spector, Nigel Walker, Susan Westmoreland, Frankie Whitman, and Bill Wilkinson. Thanks for making us smarter.

...to the friends and family who gave us access and insight into the Bay Area. To Amy Suyama of The Real Food Company: If every produce buyer had your integrity, discerning eye, and passion for agriculture, the state of small farms would be much improved. To Diane Shields for being an endless source of inspiration, humor, and great ideas. To Dan Lynch for his persistent belief in this project, for his willingness to drive to every store in Napa and Sonoma counties, and for cutting his grass for us. To Tom Graves for generously sharing his amazing contacts, his keen wit, his wonderful home, and his cellular phone. To Jim Pricco for the many miles driven, articles clipped, leads followed, and phone numbers found, and for being a kindhearted and good-natured friend. To the late Bil McManus for being the Bay Area's biggest—and most ardent—fan.

...and to the coworkers and friends at home who worked hard to make this project happen. To Palmer Uhl for her endless patience while offering technical assistance. To Jeff Slutzky for coming along at the end and cheerfully taking care of all the final minute details. To Coby Green-Rifkin for keeping us together and making us look so good. And to Michelle Speckler for always having her priorities straight, for passing that knowledge along, and for the constant reminders that Eating Fresh is the future.

They bend with determined concentration over cutting boards and saucepans, these chefs-to-be, under the watchful eye of the master. Eager to perfect the knife chop, the reduction, the emulsification, and the glaze, they learn as young painters, new ballerinas, and apprentice sculptors do: starting under the tutelage of the expert in order to master basic techniques.

Why Chefs Care about Sustainable Agriculture

Those destined to be great soon move beyond technique and enter the realm of passion for the best and freshest foods. They've quickly learned that technique alone cannot disguise mediocre culinary building blocks—the cucumber too long in transit, the wilted chard, the tomato that stays ripe (though not toothsome) for longer than nature intended.

Soon they are venturing to the fresh produce and fresh fish markets before dawn, visiting local farmers, ranchers, and fishermen to arrange for delivery of the week's just-harvested foods: squashes, lettuces, herbs, flowers, fresh-made cheeses, newly gathered shellfish, and day's-catch finfish. Early in their careers they've already sworn off mass-produced, grocery store stocks. Now they make a science of finding the best and the freshest.

They do it with conscience. Best for them is not just a fresh ingredient: it's knowing where and how that ingredient was grown and harvested; what, if anything, it was fed; how it was handled after harvest; and how much time has elapsed between harvest and kitchen. They need to know not just for the sake of taste but also out of concern for the land on which the ingredient was grown or the seas in which it swam.

Finding out means entering into what Alice Waters called the impassioned collaboration between those who produce and those who cook the ingredients. That kind of care leads the good chef—and certainly the great chef—to agriculture: to vineyards, orchards, ranches, and farms and, increasingly, to water agriculture, or aquaculture. During the search for an ingredient's source, the chef learns the difference between organically grown and chemically enhanced foods. Such a pilgrimage inevitably leads thoughtful chefs to think more deeply about the health, environmental, and cultural ramifications of the choices they make. Ultimately, it leads to new ideas, new people, and organizations that promote clean farming—sustainable farming.

Joan Dye Gussow and Kate Clancy were among the pioneers who, in a 1986 article published in the *Journal of Nutrition Education*, focused attention on the relationship between food choices and environmental sustainability. Waters brought the idea to the dining table, declaring that a restaurant can be no better than the ingredients it chooses. Waters and other chefs have since found that a search for the best ingredients proves that a good restaurant is indeed, and finally, dependent on the health of the earth and the oceans; without such searches, there simply is no best at all.

by K. Dun Gifford
President
Oldways
Preservation &
Exchange Trust
Cambridge,
Massachusetts

Few other areas in the world can match the San Francisco Bay Area for the richness and diversity of its agriculture or the quality and variety of its farm products. Within a few hundred miles of the urban center—just an hour or two's drive away—are world-class wineries; family farms growing superbly flavored fruits and vegetables year-round; numerous plant nurseries and flower farms; dairies producing acclaimed sheep, cow, and goat cheeses; outstanding specialty livestock, game bird, and poultry ranches; thriving freshwater and saltwater aquaculture operations; flourishing local fisheries; and most recently, dozens of farms producing premier olive oil.

Supporting the Agricultural Abundance of the Bay Area

Many of our regional foods are grown organically, and many have a taste of our place—what the French call *terroir*. Golden blushed, with deep-orange sweet-tart flesh, its intense flavor suggestive of bitter almond: this is unmistakably a Bay Area–grown Blenheim apricot. Sweet and delicate Dungeness crab from the chilly December ocean: this is the taste of the Bay Area New Year. Fresh sheep milk ricotta from Sonoma, with luscious Brentwood figs and tan oak honey: this says Bay Area summer.

Place and people have shaped the abundance and variety and quality of our Bay Area foods. Our region is blessed with extraordinary natural fertility, rich and diverse ecosystems, and remarkably varied soils, climates, and topographies. That native abundance was basic in the lives of the indigenous people, and its agricultural potential was evident to the first European explorers and settlers. Today our population is vital and diverse. People have come from all over the Americas, Asia, and Europe, bringing with them rich agricultural and culinary traditions.

No wonder the Bay Area has become a culinary mecca and a market center. Our renowned chefs and consumers alike have a profusion of choices with respect to where to buy the local bounty: in the nine-county Bay Area, there are over a hundred farmers markets, lots of farm stands, numerous specialty stores, hundreds of natural and organic retailers, several farm-to-consumer subscription services with enrollment in the many thousands, and now Internet food shopping services. And plans are under way for a San Francisco Public Market that will be a showcase for regional farm products and local specialty foods.

Beyond growing and marketing, many kinds of innovative education programs are helping strengthen the connection between our regional farms and our urban centers. School gardens are teaching children the relationship between healthy soil, healthy food, and healthy communities. Farm tours, agricultural tourism, and regional agricultural events offer

by Sibella Kraus
Former Executive
Director
Center for Urban
Education about
Sustainable
Agriculture
San Francisco

urban consumers the opportunity to learn firsthand about the land and people that produce their food. Regional-planning, agricultural, and food organizations help the public understand the complex issues underlying the urban-rural interdependence and help shape public policy.

Such education and policy efforts are essential, and appreciation for our regional bounty has indeed blossomed. At the same time, however, so have threats to the natural and agricultural resources on which that bounty depends. But many regional farmers are doing their part by adopting more-sustainable farming practices. Bay Area food lovers, too, are doing their part by buying local farm products and by supporting efforts to preserve our agricultural abundance as both heritage and legacy.

Resources for Living Local

The Center for Urban Education about Sustainable Agriculture

(CUESA) seeks to promote stewardship of regional sustainable agriculture among Bay Area residents through public education. The organization pursues this mission by running educational programs; by encouraging community-wide access to fresh, locally grown food; by linking rural food producers with urban consumers; and by celebrating the seasonal bounty and diversity of the Bay Area. Educational programs include Market Cooking for Kids, Shop with the Chef, Meet the Producer, and Open Garden Day, as well as management of the Ferry Plaza Farmers' Markets in San Francisco. CUESA's long-term goal is to open in San Francisco a public market and education center dedicated to sustainable agriculture.

COOKING

FRESH

from the

BAY AREA

The Bay Area's Best Recipes
for Eating Local, Organic Produce
at its Seasonal Best

ASSESSING THE STATE OF THE REGION'S SMALL FARMS AND EXPLORING WAYS TO HELP KEEP THEM VIABLE

BAY AREA WINTER CROPS

APPLES

ARUGULA

BEETS

BELGIAN ENDIVE

BLOOD ORANGES

BROCCOLI

BROCCOLI RABE

BRUSSELS SPROUTS

CABBAGE

CARROTS

CAULIFLOWER

CELERY ROOT

CHANTERELLES

CHARD

CHERVIL

CLEMENTINES

COLLARDS

DANDELION GREENS

ESCAROLE

FENNEL

FRISÉE

GRAPEFRUIT

GREEN GARLIC

KALE

KIWI

LEEKS

MÂCHE

MEYER LEMONS

MUSTARD GREENS

NAVEL ORANGES

PARSNIPS

RADICCHIO

RADISHES

RUTABAGAS

SATSUMAS

SAVOY CABBAGE

SCALLIONS

SPINACH

TURNIP GREENS

TURNIPS

WALNUTS

WATERCRESS

WILD MUSHROOMS

WINTER SQUASH

Over time I notice my own rhythms mimic those of our farm. Winter's short days allow the spirit to rest. There is time to meet, reflect, talk, and sleep. Winter allows us to store energies for the coming year. It also allows time to build and to repair things worn or broken. The parallels to tree, plant, and animal life are evident: Winter plants seem to move nutrients more slowly, accumulating and gathering in greater sweetness than at other times of year. Carrots at this time of year are turgid and crisp. Broccoli moves more slowly toward head and flower, pulling up and storing more pronounced flavors.

The Rhythm of Winter

Located two hours northeast of San Francisco in Capay Valley, Full Belly Farm has been an all-organic grower since 1983. With a menu of more than 80 crops, the farm ensures quality by selecting varieties grown not for high yield but for optimal flavor. The farm seeks not only to grow food that is mineral rich, fully flavored, and picked at its peak but also to make food and place become linked to the reality of sustainability and long-term health.

Our trees seem to reach out and up. Last season's strength and energy get stored in dense wood. The trees stand open, bare, and revealed. Branches and limbs are pocked with small leaf and fruiting buds, curled tight, closed and sleeping. The farm's soil rests. The universe of microorganisms beneath our feet metabolize and consume their food sources slowly. Cold temperatures hamper life, and wet conditions slow biological activity.

The adage that farming gets in your blood takes on clarity when I feel my very blood slowly accumulating and storing nutrients from the crops we grow and consume. The very bacteria and microbial life on leaf surface or root inoculate us with the energy of the soil from which we derive our crops. This may be as important as the vitamins and minerals contained in those crops.

Our winter workday reflects the season. Work starts at 7:30 in the morning and goes until 5 in the evening. Dawn to dark makes a respectable set of bookends for the day. Winter days contrast markedly with the longer days of summer. Stopping work in the summer becomes an act of sheer will when daylight allows for the completion of one more task.

Organic farming means more than simply chemical-free farming. Organic farming at Full Belly strives to create and support the life forces that link farmer, soil, food, fruit, animal, microbe, and consumer. We tend to get uneasy talking about life forces; the term seems on the New Age end of the vocabulary. But as I relate to this farm over the years, the notion of life force seems appropriate.

Farming is not just managing a business or pumping out food to make a profit. Healthy farming means respecting life, allowing the earth to move toward its own healthfulness, and manipulating the earth only minimally. I see it as a great positive notion that consumers who seek out healthy food also are being inoculated with Full Belly and all the life that resides here.

by Paul Muller
Full Belly Farm
Guinda, California

Community Alliance with Family Farmers is helping build a renewed agriculture that is economically viable, environmentally sound, and socially just. Its members— often from opposite sides of the economic and political fence— include activists, farmers, environmentalists, city folk, students, and gardeners. Its campaigns are actively dedicated to cultivating healthy farms, food, and communities.

by Tom Haller
Director Emeritus
Community
Alliance with
Family Farmers

Traveling the congested freeways of the San Francisco Bay Area, it's hard to imagine how family farms can survive in such a saturated urban environment. Indeed, most farms and the majority of farmland in the area were paved over years ago.

The truth is, farming in the Bay Area is not dead. In fact it's bigger than most city folk would think possible. So where are the farms? They're most visible on the edges of the region: the grape vineyards in the Napa Valley, the open pastures of Marin County, the orchards hugging the delta, the lettuce fields near Salinas, and the greenhouses and pumpkin fields near Half Moon Bay. A whole bunch of small farms—some more like large gardens—are scattered throughout the more urban areas of the region.

Bay Area Farms

Are those farms just hanging on until the consuming tentacles of development finally close around them? Maybe, but don't count them out just yet. Back in the early 1960s, some of California's leading experts predicted that small family farms would be dead by the end of that decade. They didn't count on the tenacity and inventiveness of farmers: some of the old-timers refused to sell out, and then young people began to come back to the land.

Tenacity, however, goes only so far. Through the years, the tightening screws of a worsening financial squeeze for family farmers demanded more than stubborn resistance to make a difference. The squeeze was made worse by competition between small and large farmers. Partly out of desperation and partly out of inspiration, a handful of Bay Area small farmers realized that to survive, they had to strike out on a different course from that of the big farmers in the valley.

And they did. During the past 20 or so years, those farmers developed a new approach: They produce distinctive crops that appeal to customers' tastes. They use growing techniques that are better for the environment by substituting management and labor for expensive equipment and purchased inputs. They direct and participate in the marketing of their farms' products. Specialty crops, heirloom varieties, a quality-over-quantity approach, experimentation and adoption of organic growing techniques, and direct marketing are some of the methods associated with this new type of farming. And the Bay Area is one of the places the new type of farming was first pioneered.

The aim is to produce a wide diversity of high-quality, unique foods that consumers will pay for and value. Through direct sales to consumers, stores, and restaurants in the Bay Area, farmers reach buyers by bypassing at least some aspects of the complex conventional marketing system. The bottom line is that direct sales can lead to higher farm income and to greater overall consumer satisfaction with and access to better foods.

Solutions like these, however, are not magic bullets. What has been accomplished to date is simply not enough to ensure that family farms survive. Although it is true that perhaps no other area of the United States has greater consumer support for local agriculture, that support could and should be far greater. Farmers at the area's farmers markets seldom sell all of their produce. Local restaurants and food stores that feature produce from area farms could be multiplying faster, if there was more consumer interest. And nonprofit organizations like the Community Alliance with Family Farmers would be even more successful in their education and advocacy efforts if they had greater citizen support. With that type of support, family farms in the Bay Area can thrive and society as a whole will be healthier and happier.

Farmers Markets
Citizens' Opportunity to Participate in Local Communities

by Gail Feenstra
Food Systems Coordinator Sustainable Agriculture Research and Education Program University of California, Davis

Farmers markets have flourished nationwide since regaining popularity in the 1970s. Not only have they become places where consumers can buy fresh, local, nutritious produce, but they are also places where citizens can participate in their local economies and communities.

In today's global business environment, farmers markets represent one of the few institutions that exist on a human scale. They provide a public space for consumers and producers, artisans and food businesses, and local entrepreneurs and entertainers to interact face-to-face. Here citizens can simultaneously share the goodness of the local harvest, meet and talk with their neighbors, enjoy local musicians or artists, and treat themselves to fresh bread or cinnamon rolls from the local bakery. They can engage in discussions with representatives of local services or political groups who attend the market. They can get advice about gardening or food preservation from the Master Gardener. And they can join with others in the community to celebrate the harvest, the winter holidays, the springtime, and a variety of special community events. Those opportunities for personal connections that accompany the exchange of goods and services strengthen social networks and build community vitality.

Farmers markets also build community by supporting local entrepreneurs and strengthening local businesses. They bring consumers to or near downtown areas where they are likely to do more shopping. Consumers benefit from the availability of unique products and the opportunity to offer feedback to sellers. When businesses are strong, they can provide jobs for community members, thereby contributing to a vibrant local economy.

Farmers markets have become the heart and soul of many communities. They create a sense of place. They provide a particularly enjoyable way for residents to participate in shaping their local economies and strengthening their communities. In the words of one California farmers market manager, "The farmers market improves the quality of life in this town; it creates a town center; it is the spirit of the community. The farmers market supports the agriculturally based roots from which this town has grown. It fosters cooperation and partnership among our citizens, and it gives them an opportunity to celebrate."

Buying Local Makes Good Neighbors

Most of us have had enough personal experience to appreciate that locally grown fruits and vegetables taste better than typical supermarket fare, which has been genetically reengineered, grown on monocropped megafarms, poisoned with fertilizer and pesticides, and transported 1,200 miles. When we know our food comes from farmers who use organic growing methods, we have more confidence that the food's been grown responsibly and safely. Buying local means doing business with people we know and trust. But what many of us do not fully appreciate is that buying local is good for family farmers and communities.

In 1910, for every dollar Americans spent for food, 41 cents went to farmers and 59 cents to input providers and marketers. Today 9 cents goes to farmers, 24 cents to input providers, and 67 cents to marketers.[1] Economists celebrate those statistics, because fewer farmers can grow more food for consumers not only in the United States but also worldwide. They trivialize the destruction of family farming as a regrettable but necessary cost of progress. But the costs have helped decimate once-vibrant rural communities and have increased the dependency of urban and suburban communities on food that comes from far away.

Fortunately, the emergence of a network of thriving, small-scale farms committed to organic farming raises serious questions about the cornerstone of conventional farming: economic competitiveness. Another look at the numbers suggests that community-scale production might actually lower the cost of food for local consumers. Community-scale agriculture, even if it means a slightly higher cost of farming, might help bring down the cost both of inputs—through organic growing methods—and of marketing—through local distribution. Moreover, when farmers are involved in distribution, they also have an opportunity to retain more of the value added.

This helps explain the dramatic growth of community-supported agriculture—or CSA—a system whereby families agree to pay a fee for the growing season in exchange for a box of produce each week. The contents of the box vary throughout the season; one week it may be mostly asparagus and melon; another week, potatoes and pumpkins. Some CSAs add farm products like eggs, milk, honey, herbs, flowers, and firewood. Subscribers either pick up their boxes from a nearby distribution point or have the boxes delivered to their doorsteps. Some 600 CSAs or horticultural operations—totaling 100,000 members—now exist in 42 states. A typical participating farm has about three acres, plus grazing land, and serves the needs of 60 to 100 families, who each pay roughly $400 a season. With the subscription fee paid up front, consumers share

by Michael Shuman
Institute for Economic Education and Entrepreneurship Washington, D.C.

with the farmer the risks of failure.

If you can't imagine taking a box of produce chosen by someone else but still want to support local farmers, you might want to try to shop only at community-friendly markets. Even simply asking your supermarket to carry locally grown produce is a step in the right direction. Better still, shop at stores that prioritize fruits and vegetables grown by local farmers.

Another reason a growing number of Americans are joining CSAs, are buying locally grown food directly, or are supporting supermarkets and restaurants that favor locally grown food is that they wish to help strengthen their community's economy in several different ways. First, the so-called economic multiplier is higher. If a market in, say, Montclair buys apples from a local farmer, then every purchase of apples benefits both market employees and the farmer, who in turn spends the money locally. If the apples are bought instead by mail order from, say, Washington State, most of the economic stimulus is felt thousands of miles away.

Second, tax dollars from the transaction stay local. With those same apples, a local purchase means returning a percentage to the public sector by means of the local property, sales, and income taxes paid by the store, the farmer, and the store's and the farmer's employees. That mail order transaction means both that the property and income taxes are generated primarily in the Pacific Northwest and that the sales taxes are avoided altogether. Buying local means supporting public services like schools, parks, and roads. Those public expenditures, of course, also pump up the economic multiplier.

Third, buying local helps create a more diversified economy. The more types of business there are within a region, the less economically vulnerable the region is. Green writer Kirkpatrick Sale says, "A self-sufficient town cannot be the victim of corporate-directed plant closings, or a truckers' strike, or an Arab oil boycott, or California droughts." As thousands of communities in Asia, Russia, and Brazil can now attest, becoming dependent on the global economy for food is risky. By once again localizing our community economies, we can insulate them from the tsunamis of global capital flights, deflations, and recessions.

All of these arguments underscore the economic benefits not only of buying locally grown food but also of buying it from locally owned markets. Fortunately, the choice of whether the global supermarket or a self-reliant community economy wins is, in the end, not economists'. Every time we make a purchase, we vote on whether we support globe-trotting corporations or community-friendly businesses. And if we conscientiously ignore the rhetoric of economists and vote for what's best for our communities, the future is ours.

1. Stewart Smith, "Sustainable Agriculture and Public Policy," *Maine Policy Review*, April 1993, pp. 69–70.

Resources for Living Local

Slow Food

With 60,000 members and 475 chapters in 37 countries worldwide, Slow Food is fast becoming the gourmet phenomenon of the decade. What began as a pleasure movement soon transformed into an organization dedicated to protecting and promoting regional food and drink and preserving the heritage of taste. The United States now has 2,500 members and more than 30 chapters, including eight groups in the Bay Area. Members receive a quarterly journal, four newsletters annually, and access to international events. Local events happen monthly.

What Is Community-Supported Agriculture?

Community-supported agriculture (CSA) is a connection between a local farm and those who eat the food the farm produces. Early in the season, consumers purchase shares or half shares in a local farm. Then, when the season begins, the shareholders pick up their portions of whatever is available that week. Farmers get the cash flow they need, and consumers agree to share the risks of farming in exchange for fresh, seasonal produce.

The brochure *New Town Farms* gives an excellent summary of the benefits of CSAs: In the community-supported farm structure, every member of the relationship benefits: the shareholders, the farmers, the farm (the earth), and the greater community.

The shareholders:
- Receive fresh, contamination-free vegetables and herbs delivered on the day of harvest.
- Pay close-to-supermarket prices for fresh, certified-organic produce.
- Know where and how their food is grown and who grows it and have the opportunity to partake in the miracle of the growing of food.
- Are provided with a structure whereby they can support a viable local agriculture, preserve local farmland, and contribute to a healthy local economy.
- Have the opportunity to gain knowledge of the growing of food and the stewardship of the earth.
- Become more aware of their relation to the land, farm life, and processes that make our lives possible.

The farmers:
- Are given the opportunity to make a viable income by growing food in a responsible and harmonious way, directly supported by the consumer—no middleman.
- Have the pleasure of knowing to whom their products are going and consequently, feel more care, responsibility, and reward in their work.
- Are relieved of marketing labor and can focus more on growing food.

The farm:
- Is preserved from development and from harmful farming practices.
- Is nurtured into a fertile, bountiful land.

The greater community:
- Benefits by the preservation of open spaces and the maintaining of an important agricultural component in an area that is rapidly being consumed by development and industry and by preserving that diversity, becomes a more whole and more satisfying place to live.
- Is strengthened by bringing together those who share healthy concerns about the future.
- And the local economy are boosted when food dollars remain within the community rather than support out-of-state corporations.

Robyn Van En, a pioneer in bringing the CSA movement to the United States, summed it up this way: food producers plus food consumers plus an annual commitment to one another equals CSA and untold possibilities. The essence of the relationship is a mutual commitment: the farm feeds the people, and the people support the farm and share the inherent risks and potential bounty.

by Elizabeth Henderson

Excerpts from Sharing the Harvest: A Guide to Community Supported Agriculture *by Elizabeth Henderson with Robyn Van En, Chelsea Green, March 1999*

Picture this: You stop at your local farm stand for a dozen ears of corn. You pull out a $10 bill and lo and behold, instead of Thomas Jefferson staring back at you, it's a head of cabbage. Sound strange? It is, unless you happen to buy your produce in the rural Berkshires of western Massachusetts. Here, family farmers have taken to issuing their own money—called Farm Preserve notes—in an effort to boost their local GNP (great natural produce).

Communities That Grow Their Own Money

When Donald and Ruth Zeigler's roadside farm store burned down and Dan and Martha Tawczynski were struggling to pay their greenhouse's heating bill, they turned not to their banks but to their customers. With the help of Susan Witt at the E. F. Schumacher Society, a nearby community economics resource center, they designed and printed their cabbage-faced notes in $10 denominations, which they sold for $9 each. Folks who purchased them agreed to wait until the growing season before redeeming them for $10 worth of produce each.

The $7,000 raised by Farm Preserve notes that first year buoyed balance books and community pride. "It would have been impossible to survive without the notes," says Dan Tawczynski, who, along with the Zeiglers, has kept them rolling off the press for several years now. Customers now used to the special, hand-illustrated green-and-tan notes in their wallets say they appreciate saving 10 percent on fruits and vegetables and preserving a way of life that sustains themselves and their neighbors.

For most of us, money flows almost unconsciously through our lives and even more imperceptibly, connects us to the lives of people and places around the globe. But for folks like the Tawczynskis and the Zeiglers, money is making a deliberate and personal homecoming. For reasons both practical and philosophical, they're issuing it themselves. And what's more, it's entirely legal, as long as they don't copy Uncle Sam's greenbacks. It also continues a long tradition of locally issued money in the United States.

Not far from the Berkshires, along the banks of the Connecticut River, a network of hundreds of businesses and individuals called the Valley Trade Connection (VTC) has issued nearly $60,000 of its own currency, known as Valley dollars. The group was created in 1991 by a small circle of women banding together to cope with frozen wages by exchanging their time and talents. Later expanding into the wider Pioneer Valley region, they introduced the dollar-size blue notes, printed in $1, $5, $10, and $20 denominations on local paper made from recycled blue jeans. Adorned with regional scenes and wildlife, and the moniker *In Community We Trust*, VTC members use Valley dollars alongside greenbacks and old-fashioned barter to exchange the nearly 1,000 locally produced or supplied

by Tim Cohen-Mitchell
Valley Trade Connection Greenfield, Massachusetts

goods and services listed in the group's directory, ranging from accounting to zipper repair.

The VTC is one of more than 60 community currency groups that have sprung up in North America in recent years. Most are modeled on Ithaca HOURS, a network of some 1,500 traders launched in 1991 by community economist Paul Glover, in Ithaca, New York. "The beauty of community currency is that it's money with a boundary around it," says Glover. Community currency helps community members hire each other and recycle the value of those exchanges within the area. A baby-sitter spends her HOURS at the deli. The deli spends them on pickles at the farmers market. The pickle maker uses them at the movies. The movie house spends them on newspaper advertising. The newspaper donates them to the YMCA. The YMCA hires the baby-sitter. And on it goes.

A means of exchange, money also can be a means for building community. In a global economy, such intimacy is difficult if not impossible. The tomatoes we buy at the supermarket may be ferried there—half ripe and refrigerated—from an anonymous, far-flung field and grower and rung up by an unfamiliar, harried cashier. But for Witt, the juicy, ripe specimen we buy at the local farm stand may send us home with more than a delicious tomato: "We bring along a story, a memory, and a connection to the people and places that make up our community." And we'll know that if we used "local tender" to make our purchase, our money will continue its rounds, bringing these same gifts to our neighbors.

Resources for Living Local

Berkeley Region Exchange and Development (BREAD) is a local currency in and around Berkeley, California. Members of BREAD agree to accept and spend BREAD Hours in exchange for local goods and services, such as bicycle repairs, housecleaning, legal services, computer consulting, massages, clerical work, carpentry, and household repairs. The local money is valued in hours because it's backed by members' labor. The ideas are to start valuing each others' work more equally and to keep the money in the local community.

GRILLED RADICCHIO WITH BALSAMIC MAYONNAISE
Judy Rodgers, Zuni 14

PORK CHOPS BRAISED WITH RED CABBAGE & APPLES
Bradley Ogden, Lark Creek Inn 15

WINTER SWEET POTATO & CONFIT OF DUCK NAPOLEON WITH RAPINI
George Cronk, Park Grill 16

ROASTED ACORN SQUASH, PEARS & POTATOES WITH BUCHERON CHEESE
Jody Denton, Restaurant LuLu 18

WINTER SQUASH-PEAR SOUP WITH TARRAGON CREAM
Eric Tucker, Millennium 19

SAGE & MILK BRINED PORK LOIN WITH CAVOLO NERO
Reed Hearon, Rose Pistola 20

SAVORY PARSNIP MUFFINS
David Kinch, Restaurant Sent Sovi 22

HALIBUT FILLET WITH LEMON-MUSHROOM SAUCE
Dan Berman, Mixx 23

PERSIMMON PUDDING WITH CRÈME ANGLAISE
Gary Danko, Gary Danko 24

SHOULDER OF LAMB BRAISED IN CHIANTI
Paul Bertolli, Oliveto 26

MEYER LEMON & HAZELNUT MERINGUE TART
Wendy Brucker, Rivoli 28

CONSOMMÉ OF SHIITAKE MUSHROOMS & JULIENNE VEGETABLES
Daniel Patterson, Elisabeth Daniel 30

PEAR & POMEGRANATE SALAD WITH WALNUT VINAIGRETTE & BALSAMIC GLAZE
Thomas Vinolus, Bittersweet Bistro 31

RISOTTO CAKES WITH FOREST MUSHROOMS & CELERY ROOT CHIPS
Ralph Tingle, Bistro Ralph 32

WINTER SQUASH SOUP WITH SWEET POTATO RELISH
Nancy Oakes, Boulevard 34

MANY-VEGETABLE PASTA WITH FETA CHEESE
Jesse Cool, Flea Street Café 36

WINTER VEGETABLES & WHITE BEAN RAGOUT
Annie Somerville, Greens 38

ROASTED TENDERLOIN OF BEEF WITH CHANTERELLE BREAD PUDDING
& WARM TREVISO SALAD
Anne Gingrass, Hawthorne Lane 40

EMPANADA STUFFED WITH DUCK CONFIT & CHANTERELLE MUSHROOMS
Frances Wilson, Lalime's 42

CELERIAC & APPLE SOUP WITH ST. GEORGE CHEESE TOASTS
Frances Wilson, Lalime's 43

CORIANDER-CURED LAMB WITH DRIED CHERRY-ZINFANDEL SAUCE
& BASIL MASHED POTATOES
Michael Quigley, Cafe Lolo 44

Winter Recipes

Martin Bournhonesque, the indefatigable farmer at Pomponio Creek, supplies Zuni — and a few other lucky Bay Area restaurants — with a gorgeous bouquet of three different radicchii throughout the winter: the most familiar red radicchio, a speckled ruby-and-green Castelfranco variety, and Medusa-like heads of Treviso. We mix them raw in salads, but they are also stunning grilled, or arrayed on a wide platter as a first course, or offered as a side dish with grilled birds, fish, beef, or lamb.

Grilled Radicchio
with Balsamic Mayonnaise

SERVES 4

Offer the grilled radicchio with this mayonnaise:

2 raw egg yolks (see note on page 175)

2 salted anchovy fillets, rinsed, patted dry, and finely chopped

1 teaspoon hot Dijon-style mustard

1 to 3 tablespoons balsamic vinegar

1½ to 2 cups mild olive oil

3 nine-minute eggs, chopped

Fine sea salt

2 heads radicchio

Olive oil

1. Light the grill.

2. Just before you grill the radicchii, make the mayonnaise. Place the yolks in a deep bowl with the anchovies, the mustard, and 1 tablespoon of the balsamic. Whisk together and then add the olive oil, a few dribbles at first, whisking evenly until it is absorbed. Gradually increase the flow until the mayonnaise is thick but not pasty. Stir in the chopped egg and season with sea salt. Taste and add more balsamic if you like. Refrigerate any leftover mayonnaise.

3. To grill the radicchii, wash the heads, removing and discarding damaged or wilted outer leaves. Cut into halves or quarters if they are large. Toss them gently with olive oil and fine sea salt. Grill quickly over a hot fire, turning only once—don't fuss with them—and the outer leaves will grill to a nice, slightly charred delicacy with a sweet, tobacco-y aRoma and taste.

Chef's Recommendation: Merlot

Zuni
San Francisco
Judy Rodgers
Chef/Owner

Pork Chops Braised with Red Cabbage & Apples

SERVES 4

4 rib-cut pork chops, 1 inch thick (see note in sidebar)

Kosher salt

Fresh cracked black pepper

¼ cup diced onion

¼ cup diced carrot

¼ cup diced celery

1 small head red cabbage, quartered, cored, and sliced ¼ inch thick

2 medium cooking apples, peeled, cored, and diced

1 clove garlic, unpeeled

6 sprigs fresh thyme, leaves stripped from the stem (or ⅓ teaspoon dried)

½ bay leaf

1 cup dry white wine or chicken stock (see page 71)

2 tablespoons balsamic vinegar

¼ cup Mustard Thyme Butter (see sidebar)

1. Trim excess fat from the pork chops, leaving about ⅛ inch around the edges. Place the trimmings in a heavy-bottomed skillet that is large enough to eventually hold all the pork chops. Cook the trimmings over low heat to render (melt) the fat. Remove the browned pieces and use the rendered fat to lightly coat the skillet. Increase the heat to moderate and brown the pork chops well on both sides. Remove and season with salt and pepper.

2. Sauté onion, carrot, and celery in the pork drippings for 5 minutes. Add the cabbage, apple, garlic, thyme, and bay leaf. Sauté for another 5 minutes or until the cabbage has wilted. Season with salt and pepper and add the white wine or stock and the balsamic vinegar.

3. Arrange the pork chops in the pan and baste with the cabbage and its juices. Reduce the heat, cover, and cook slowly for about 45 minutes, turning and basting once or twice, until the pork chops are tender. Be careful that the liquid never boils while the pork chops are in the pan or they will be tough.

4. To serve, remove the garlic and bay leaf and arrange the cabbage on hot serving plates. Place a pork chop on each plate and top each with a dollop of Mustard Thyme Butter. *Chef's Recommendation: Syrah, Edmund St. John, "Durell," Sonoma or MacTarnahan's Amber Ale*

Make this with rib chops that have a little fat. Loin chops are too lean for this recipe and will become tough and dry.

Mustard Thyme Butter

makes ½ cup

6 tablespoons unsalted butter, at room temperature

1 tablespoon fresh thyme, chopped

3 tablespoons Dijon mustard

½ teaspoon kosher salt

¼ teaspoon fresh cracked pepper

Juice of ½ lemon

Combine all the ingredients in a small bowl. Cover and refrigerate. Serve at room temperature.

Lark Creek Inn
Larkspur
Bradley Ogden
Chef/Co-owner

Sweet Potato Cakes

1 pound sweet potatoes

$^1/_4$ cup diced onion

1 teaspoon minced garlic

2 tablespoons flour

$^1/_4$ cup oatmeal

1 egg

$^1/_2$ teaspoon salt

$^1/_4$ teaspoon pepper

3 tablespoons olive oil

Preheat oven to 400°F.

Peel the sweet potatoes and, using a box grater, grate into a bowl. Add the onion, garlic, flour, oatmeal, egg, salt, and

(continued next page)

⸬ PARK GRILL ⸬

Park Hyatt San Francisco
San Francisco
George Cronk
Former Executive Chef

Winter Sweet Potato & Confit of Duck Napoleon with Rapini

SERVES 4

4 duck legs

$^1/_2$ teaspoon cracked black pepper

1 teaspoon kosher salt

$^1/_4$ teaspoon fresh thyme

$^1/_2$ teaspoon chopped bay leaf

3 tablespoons olive oil

3 cups Rendered Duck Fat (see next page)

$^1/_2$ carrot, chopped

1 celery stalk, chopped

$^1/_4$ onion, chopped

3 cloves garlic, chopped rough

1$^1/_2$ cups chicken stock

4 tablespoons unsalted butter

$^1/_4$ teaspoon salt

$^1/_4$ teaspoon pepper

For the rapini:

2 tablespoons butter

$^1/_4$ teaspoon minced garlic

4 ounces broccoli rabe, trimmed and blanched

$^1/_2$ teaspoon salt

$^1/_8$ teaspoon pepper

Sweet Potato Cakes (see sidebar)

Two days before cooking:

1. Clean duck legs of silver skin and excess fat. Sprinkle each duck leg top and bottom with pepper, salt, thyme, and bay leaf. Place legs on a wire rack, fat side down. Place the rack on a baking sheet and cover loosely with a dry dishcloth. Do not use plastic wrap. Refrigerate for 2 days.

The day of the meal:

2. Preheat oven to 250°F.

3. Wipe the herbs off the duck legs. Heat the olive oil in a medium-size skillet or sauté pan. The pan should be very hot. Sear the duck legs on both sides and remove from the heat.

4. Heat the duck fat in a pan large enough to hold the duck legs and the vegetables. Bring the duck fat to simmer and place the duck legs, carrot, celery, onion, and garlic in the fat. They should be completely covered in duck fat. Cover and put in the oven for approximately 2½ hours or until tender. Pull legs from the oven. Carefully remove them from fat and let stand. When cool enough to handle, pull the meat from the duck legs.

5. Boil the chicken stock until it is reduced by half. Whisk in pieces of cold butter. Season with salt and pepper.

6. To prepare the rapini, heat the butter and toss in garlic to sweat. Add the blanched broccoli rabe and cook until tender. Season with salt and pepper.

7. To assemble, place one potato cake in the center of each plate. Around the top, place about 4 ounces of duck confit. Put the broccoli rabe on top of the duck and sauce with the reduced chicken stock.

Chef's Recommendation: Pinot Noir, Robert Sinskey 1996

Rendered Duck Fat

recipe by Joseph George
yield: approximately 3 cups
3 pounds duck skin and fat
3 cups water

Dice the skin and fat and combine it with the water in a small saucepan. Bring the liquid to a slow simmer. Skim any impurities that may rise to the surface. Simmer the fat slowly for 1½ to 2 hours or until all of the water has evaporated and the fat has clarified. You will be able to tell when the fat is rendered by the way it looks: it will be very clear and the simmering bubbles will be much smaller. Strain the fat through a fine-mesh colander or cheesecloth and discard the skin. Rendered fat can be refrigerated for 2 months or frozen for up to 1 year.

(Sweet Potato Cakes continued)

pepper. Stir to combine and form the mixture into small, 3- to 3½-ounce cakes.

Heat a medium-size skillet or sauté pan to the smoking point and coat with olive oil. Sear the cakes on both sides and finish by placing them in the oven for 8 to 10 minutes. They should be firm when you press them. Let stand.

Roasted Acorn Squash, Pears & Potatoes
with Bucheron Cheese

SERVES 6 TO 8

1 acorn squash, cut in 8 wedges, seeds removed

1 pound fingerling or other small potatoes, washed thoroughly

1 pound cipolinni or other small onion

3 tablespoons extra virgin olive oil

Salt and pepper

16 cloves garlic, peels left on

1 pear, cut into eight wedges

4 sprigs fresh thyme

2 tablespoons LuLu Fig Balsamic Vinegar

$^1/_2$ cup Bucheron or other aged goat cheese

$^1/_4$ cup hazelnuts, toasted and chopped

1. Preheat oven to 375°F.

2. In a large mixing bowl, toss the acorn squash, potatoes, and onions with 2 tablespoons of the olive oil and a little salt and pepper. Lay them out evenly on a baking sheet or in a large casserole dish and place them in the oven.

3. After about 30 minutes, coat the garlic cloves in $^1/_2$ tablespoon of the olive oil and a little salt and pepper and scatter over the roasting vegetables. Return to the oven.

4. After 10 minutes more, toss the pear and thyme with the remaining $^1/_2$ tablespoon of olive oil and a little salt and pepper and distribute evenly over the pan of roasting vegetables. Return to the oven for another 15 minutes.

5. Arrange the hot vegetables on a large platter, drizzle with LuLu Fig Balsamic Vinegar, and crumble the goat cheese over the top. Place the entire platter in the oven for 2 or 3 minutes, just to lightly melt the cheese. Sprinkle the hazelnuts over the top and serve immediately.

Chef's Recommendation: Syrah

Restaurant LuLu
San Francisco
Jody Denton
Chef/Partner

Winter Squash-Pear Soup
with Tarragon Cream

SERVES 8

¹/₂ cup white wine or sherry

2 yellow onions, cut in half and sliced thin

2 cups diced celery

3 pears

3- to 4-pound butternut or kuri squash, peeled and diced into 1-inch cubes

1 teaspoon dried tarragon

1 teaspoon dried thyme

2¹/₂ quarts light vegetable stock

¹/₃ cup white miso

1 teaspoon salt

¹/₂ teaspoon black pepper

Tarragon Cream (see sidebar)

1. Heat the wine or sherry in a soup pot and add the onions and celery. Cook the vegetables over medium heat until the liquid evaporates and the onions are lightly browned.

2. Peel, core, and dice 2 of the pears into 1-inch cubes. Add the pear, squash, tarragon, thyme, and vegetable stock to the soup pot. Bring to a boil over medium-high heat, turn down the heat, and simmer, covered, over a medium flame until the squash is soft, about 40 minutes.

3. Puree the soup with the miso in batches in a food processor or blender until smooth. Return the soup to the pot and add the salt and pepper.

4. Slice the remaining pear into very thin slices. Ladle the soup into bowls and top with tarragon cream and pear slices.

Chef's Recommendation: dry Riesling or Gewürztraminer

Tarragon Cream

1 cup cashews

¹/₄ cup fresh tarragon leaves

2 cups water

Juice of 2 lemons

¹/₃ teaspoon nutmeg

1 teaspoon salt

Place all of the ingredients into a blender and blend until very smooth. If still gritty, strain through a chinois (fine strainer) or cheesecloth.

Millennium
San Francisco
Eric Tucker
Head Chef

Sage & Milk Brined Pork Loin
with Cavolo Nero

SERVES 4

8 cloves garlic

12 sage leaves

$^1/_2$ tablespoon salt

$1^1/_2$ tablespoons ground black pepper

$^1/_2$ gallon milk

4 pork chops, uncut in a single rack

4 bunches cavolo nero (also called black kale or lascinata kale)

$^1/_3$ cup extra virgin olive oil

1 onion, peeled and diced

2 sprigs marjoram

$^1/_2$ teaspoon salt

$^1/_4$ teaspoon black pepper

2 lemons (preferably Meyer lemons) cut in wedges

The day before cooking:

1. Using a mortar and pestle, pound together 6 of the garlic cloves, the sage, and salt (or puree the garlic, sage, and salt in a food processor with the milk). Place the pounded mixture in a glass or stainless steel pan large enough to hold the pork loin. Add the pepper and milk and stir until well mixed.

2. Add the pork loin to the pan and coat it with the marinade. Cover with plastic wrap and marinate in the refrigerator for at least 24 hours.

The day of cooking:

3. Preheat oven to 400°F.

4. Wash the kale thoroughly and remove the leaves from the large stems. Discard the stems and cut the kale into 1-inch pieces. Lightly crush the 2 remaining garlic cloves to release their juices.

Rose Pistola

Rose Pistola
San Francisco
Reed Hearon
Chef/Owner

5. Heat a large skillet and add the olive oil. Sauté the onion, crushed garlic cloves, and marjoram until the onion and garlic are translucent. Add the kale to the pan, and stir to coat with olive oil and seasonings. Stir in 1/2 cup of water. Bring to a boil and then lower the heat and simmer, covered, until tender, approximately 20 minutes. Stir often to avoid scorching. Remove the pan from the heat and reserve.

6. Remove the pork loin from the marinade and pat it dry with absorbent towel. Season the pork loin with the remaining 1/2 teaspoon salt and 1/4 teaspoon pepper. Place the pork in a small roasting pan or an appropriately sized ovenproof skillet. Roast the pork for approximately 45 minutes or until the internal temperature reads 165°F on an instant-read thermometer. Halfway through cooking the pork, squeeze the juice of 1 lemon across it and add the squeezed wedges to the pan.

7. Once the pork is cooked, remove the pan from the oven. Cover the pork with a clean kitchen towel or aluminum foil and allow it to rest for 10 to 15 minutes.

8. To serve, carve the pork into 4 pieces by cutting between the bones. Gently reheat the braised kale over medium heat. Divide the kale onto 4 warmed dinner plates, place a pork chop on top of the kale, and garnish with the remaining lemon wedges.

Chef's Recommendation: Chianti Classico, Poggerino 1996

Parsnip Puree

12 ounces parsnips, peeled & sliced

1 bay leaf

1 tablespoon sugar

½ teaspoon salt

2 cups whole milk

Combine the parsnips, bay leaf, sugar, salt, and milk in a small saucepan. Bring to a boil, lower the heat, and simmer for about 10 minutes or until the parsnips are very soft. Don't be concerned if the milk separates and clumps up. Remove the bay leaf from the milk and transfer the milk-parsnip mixture to a blender or food processor. Puree until smooth and allow the pureed parsnips to cool to room temperature.

**Restaurant
Sent Sovi**
Saratoga
David Kinch
Chef/Owner

Savory Parsnip Muffins

MAKES ABOUT 18 MUFFINS

½ pound unsalted butter, plus extra to line the muffin tins

2 eggs plus 1 egg yolk

Parsnip Puree (see sidebar)

1½ cups all-purpose flour, plus extra to line the muffin tins

1 teaspoon baking soda

½ teaspoon baking powder

2 teaspoons salt

2 tablespoons sugar

¼ teaspoon black pepper

1 teaspoon fresh thyme, minced (or ½ teaspoon dried)

1. Preheat oven to 375°F.

2. Prepare the muffin tins by lining them with butter, then dusting them with flour. Shake any excess flour from the tins.

3. Place the butter in a bowl large enough to hold all the ingredients and beat with an electric mixer until fluffy and noticeably lighter in color, about 3 minutes. Add the eggs and the egg yolk and beat for an additional 2 minutes. On low speed, add the parsnip puree and mix thoroughly. Add the flour, baking soda, baking powder, salt, sugar, black pepper, and thyme. Mix for 1 minute or until all of the ingredients are completely incorporated. Do not overmix.

4. Fill each cup in the muffin pan halfway full with the mix. Tap the pan lightly on a table to remove air bubbles. Bake the muffins until they have doubled in size, are brown on top, and begin to pull away from the sides of the tin, about 20 minutes. Remove the pan from the oven, and the muffins from the tin. Place the muffins on a wire cooling rack or clean kitchen towel to cool. Allow the muffins to rest for 10 minutes before serving.

Chef's Recommendation: Pinot Noir, J. Swan, Sonoma 1996

Halibut Fillet with Lemon-Mushroom Sauce

SERVES 2

1 tablespoon peanut oil (or other hot-burning oil)

2 six-ounce halibut fillets

Salt and freshly ground white pepper to taste

2 tablespoons flour

1 tablespoon unsalted butter

4 ounces chanterelle or wild mushrooms, sliced

1/2 teaspoon finely diced garlic

1/2 teaspoon finely diced shallots

1/4 cup Chardonnay

1/4 cup fish stock (or light chicken stock)

1/2 cup heavy cream

Zest and juice of 1 lemon

1 teaspoon finely minced parsley

1. Heat oil in hot skillet until almost smoking. Season fish with salt and pepper; dust lightly with flour, gently shaking off excess. Place fish in skillet and sauté until golden, about 2 minutes. Carefully turn fish over with a broad spatula and sauté another 2 minutes until golden. Remove from pan, place on plate, cover, and keep warm.

2. Pour off excess oil in skillet. Add butter and allow to bubble, but do not let brown. Add mushrooms and sauté over medium heat until they render juices. Add garlic and shallots; sauté until soft and translucent, 1 to 2 minutes. Add Chardonnay, bring to a boil, and reduce by half, about 2 minutes. Add fish stock, boil, and reduce by half, about 2 minutes. Gradually add cream, stirring constantly. Bring to the boiling point, lower heat, and simmer, stirring frequently to reduce mixture until it lightly coats the back of a spoon. Slowly add 1 tablespoon lemon juice and the parsley, and season with salt and pepper to taste.

3. To serve, place halibut fillet on two warm plates. Divide sauce evenly and diagonally across fish. Garnish with lemon zest.

Chef's Recommendation: Chardonnay, Sonoma-Cutrer "Cutrer Vineyard," Sonoma Coast 1996

Mixx
Santa Rosa
Dan Berman
Chef/Proprietor

*Select fresh,
completely ripe
Hachiya persim-
mons. The skin
color should be
deep and vibrant;
the flesh should be
soft, jellylike, and
translucent. Peel,
seed, and in a food
processor or
blender, process
until smooth.*

Persimmon Pudding
with Crème Anglaise

*This pudding may be made several days ahead of time and slowly reheated
in a 300°F oven just before serving.*

SERVES 8

1 teaspoon freshly ground cinnamon

1 teaspoon freshly grated or ground nutmeg

1 teaspoon baking soda

1/2 teaspoon salt

1 1/2 cups flour, sifted

2 cups puree, made from Hachiya persimmons (see sidebar)

2 eggs

1 cup light brown sugar

1/2 cup melted sweet butter

1 teaspoon vanilla extract

1 cup light cream or half-and-half

Crème Anglaise (see next page)

1. Preheat oven to 350°F.

2. Butter a 9- x 3-inch round cake pan or springform pan with tight seal.

3. Sift together cinnamon, nutmeg, baking soda, salt, and flour. In a
   separate bowl, whisk together persimmon puree, eggs, sugar, melted
   butter, vanilla, and cream. Stir in flour mixture and whisk well to
   combine.

4. Pour batter into the pan and cover tightly with foil (shiny side to the
   batter). Create a water bath by sitting the cake pan in a casserole and
   adding water until it comes about halfway up the outside of the cake
   pan. Bake for 2 to 2 1/2 hours or until a skewer comes out clean. Let cool
   to lukewarm and serve with Crème Anglaise.

Chef's Recommendation: Tokaiji Aszn, 6 Puttonyos, Oremus, Hungary 1992

GARY DANKO

Gary Danko
San Francisco
Gary Danko
Chef/Owner

Crème Anglaise

4 egg yolks

4 tablespoons sugar

Pinch salt

1 cup light cream or half-and-half

1/2 vanilla bean, scraped

1. *In a heavy, medium-size saucepan, combine and whisk the egg yolks, sugar, and salt. Set aside.*

2. *Place cream in a small saucepan and bring to the boiling point, but do not boil. Add scraped vanilla bean seeds and, stirring constantly, infuse for several minutes.*

3. *Whisk the hot cream into the reserved egg mixture. Place over medium heat and cook, stirring constantly, thoroughly but gently, until the custard coats the back of a spoon. Be careful that the sauce does not boil.*

4. *Remove from the heat, stir gently once or twice to smooth, and strain through a fine-mesh sieve.*

5. *Cool in a bowl over ice and when completely chilled, refrigerate until needed.*

Shoulder of Lamb Braised in Chianti

SERVES 8

3 pounds boneless shoulder of spring lamb, cut into pieces
    roughly 1 inch square

1½ teaspoons salt

½ teaspoon black pepper

3 tablespoons olive oil

1 carrot, peeled and finely diced

1 small stalk celery, finely diced

1 shallot, peeled and diced

1 head garlic, peeled

6 sprigs fresh thyme

2 tablespoons flour

5 cups Chianti

1 tablespoon red wine vinegar

1. Place the lamb on a sheet pan and season it with the salt and pepper.

2. Over medium-high heat, heat the olive oil in a heavy, wide-bottomed pot that is large enough to cook the meat in a single layer. When the oil is very hot, add the lamb. Brown the meat well on all sides and remove it from the pan. (If your pot is not large enough to cook the lamb in one layer, brown the meat in batches.)

3. Add the carrots, celery, shallots, garlic cloves, and thyme to the pan and cook them over low heat until they are soft. Use a wooden spoon to loosen any bits of meat or vegetable that may be sticking to the bottom of the pan.

4. Add the meat back to the pan and sprinkle with the flour. Stir the flour into the meat and vegetables and continue to cook the mixture over low heat for about 5 to 8 minutes. Raise the heat to medium high and add the wine (the wine should barely cover the meat). Bring the liquid to a slow simmer (do not let it boil), lower the heat, and cover the pot. Cook the lamb for 1½ to 2 hours or until it is tender.

Oliveto

Oliveto
Oakland
Paul Bertolli
Chef/Owner

5. Remove the lamb from the sauce and discard the thyme. Puree the vegetables with the garlic and sauce in a food mill, food processor, or blender and return the mixture to the pot. Check the consistency of the sauce; it should be viscous enough to coat the back of a wooden spoon—not at all runny. If the sauce seems too thin, simmer it on the stove until it thickens. Finish the sauce by stirring in the red wine vinegar.

6. Return the lamb to the pan and warm it gently over medium heat. Do not let it boil. Serve on warm plates or in wide-brimmed bowls.

Note: It is best to make this dish at least 8 hours ahead to allow the flavors to fully steep into the sauce.

Chef's Recommendation: Brunello di Montalcino, Tarenti 1993

Meyer Lemon & Hazelnut Meringue Tart

SERVES 8 TO 10

For the tart:

3 eggs, separated

$^3/_4$ cup sugar

Grated zest of 1 large Meyer lemon

1 teaspoon vanilla extract

1 cup finely ground hazelnuts

1 cup finely ground almonds

$1^1/_2$ tablespoons flour

$^1/_4$ teaspoon salt

For the meringue:

2 Meyer lemons (include the peeled lemon used in the tart)

4 large egg whites

$1^1/_4$ cups sugar

Powdered sugar for garnish

1. Preheat oven to 350°F.

2. Line a 10-inch round cake pan or springform pan with parchment, and butter lightly. Dust with a fine coat of flour, and shake out excess.

3. Whisk together 3 egg yolks and sugar until pale and fluffy. Add lemon zest and vanilla, whisking well until mixture regains fluffiness.

4. Mix together hazelnuts and almonds. Combine 1 cup of this ground nut mixture with the flour. Reserve remaining nuts for meringue.

5. Beat 3 egg whites until foamy. Sprinkle in salt and continue beating until soft peaks form. In alternating thirds, gently fold the nut-flour mixture and whites into the egg yolk mixture. Pour into prepared pan. Bake 25 to 30 minutes until lightly browned. Set aside to cool on a rack for 15 minutes. Run a knife around the edge of the pan to loosen, invert onto a plate, and remove parchment. Cool.

Rivoli
Berkeley
Wendy Brucker
Chef/Owner

6. Reduce oven to 300°F.

7. To prepare meringue, peel the remaining lemon and remove the membrane from the segments of both lemons, working over a bowl to catch their juice. Squeeze remaining juice out of the cores. Arrange lemon segments over cooled cake and drizzle with juice.

8. Whisk egg whites until foamy. Gradually add sugar, whisking continuously, until stiff peaks form and the mixture is thick and shiny. This takes about 10 minutes of beating at high speed with an electric mixer.

9. Gently fold in reserved nuts. Spread meringue evenly over cake and bake for 30 minutes. Meringue may crack as it dries, and that's OK. Cool on a rack. Dust with powdered sugar. Slice and serve.

Chef's Recommendation: Muscat Beaumes de Venise

Cowgirl Creamery creates batches of fresh, handmade, organic cheeses daily. In the tradition of on-farm cheese-making in the French countryside, Cowgirl Creamery focuses on fresh cheeses sold regionally. The cheeses are made exclusively with certified organic milk from the Straus Family Creamery. Cowgirl Creamery is located one hour north of San Francisco in Point Reyes Station.

Garnish

Olive oil

Salt

5 shiitake caps

3 ounces each carrot, leek, and celery root, cut into 2-inch pieces and finely julienned

Preheat oven to 350°F. Lightly oil and salt the shiitake caps, lay them out on a baking sheet, and roast for 15 minutes. Once cooled, julienne and set aside. Cook the carrots, leeks, and celery root separately in heavily salted boiling water until just tender. Refresh under cold running water and drain. Combine the julienned vegetables and mushrooms.

restaurant
ELISABETH DANIEL

Elisabeth Daniel
San Francisco
Daniel Patterson
Chef/Owner

Consommé of Shiitake Mushrooms & Julienne Vegetables

SERVES 6

2½ pounds shiitake mushrooms, cleaned and coarsely chopped

1 large carrot, peeled and sliced

½ large onion, sliced

½ large onion, charred over an open flame

⅓ cup peeled and sliced celery root

½ head of fennel, sliced

1 leek, sliced

⅓ bunch thyme

½ teaspoon black peppercorns

½ ounce dried cèpes (also called porcini mushrooms)

Salt

Garnish (see sidebar)

Chive oil (optional)

1. Preheat oven to 450°F.

2. On 2 very lightly oiled sheet pans, spread out the shiitakes evenly and, stirring every few minutes, roast until lightly browned, about 15 to 20 minutes. After removing mushrooms, add 1 cup of warm water to each sheet pan. Let stand for 2 minutes and then scrape up any bits of browned mushroom on the bottom of each pan.

3. Put the mushrooms, liquid, carrot, onion, celery root, fennel, leek, thyme, peppercorns, and cèpes into a nonreactive stockpot. Cover with water by about 1 inch. Add salt and bring to a slow simmer. Let cook for 3 hours.

4. Strain through a fine-mesh sieve lined with cheesecloth or a cloth napkin. Season with salt, if necessary.

5. Divide the garnish among 6 soup plates and heat plates in a 350°F oven for 1 minute. Ladle consommé into each bowl and drizzle with chive oil.

Chef's Recommendation: Amontillado Escadrilla Sherry, E. Lustav

Pear & Pomegranate Salad
with Walnut Vinaigrette & Balsamic Glaze

SERVES 8

1 cup walnuts, toasted and chopped roughly

1 tablespoon Dijon mustard

1 tablespoon honey

2 tablespoons lemon juice, freshly squeezed

2 tablespoons champagne vinegar

1/2 cup walnut oil

Salt and white pepper to taste

4 tablespoons powdered sugar

4 pears—Bosc, Comice, or Bartlett—cored and cut into 1/4-inch wedges

1 pound mesclun greens

1 cup pomegranate seeds from 3 whole pomegranates

6 ounces Roquefort cheese

Balsamic Glaze (see sidebar)

1. Preheat oven to 550°F.

2. To make the vinaigrette, use a food processor to puree 1/2 cup of the walnuts along with the mustard, honey, lemon juice, and vinegar. While the processor is running, slowly add the oil. Season with salt and white pepper to taste.

3. Sift half of the powdered sugar onto a rimmed baking pan to coat evenly. Lay wedges of pear on the pan in a single layer and sift the remaining sugar on top of the pears. Bake until the sugar on the pan caramelizes (dark golden brown) and the pears are cooked.

4. Toss mesclun greens with vinaigrette in a large bowl. Divide among 8 chilled plates and top with roasted pears, pomegranate seeds, the remaining walnuts, and Roquefort cheese. Drizzle with Balsamic Glaze. Serve immediately.

Chef's Recommendation: Pinot Noir Reserve, Morgan

Balsamic Glaze

1 cup balsamic vinegar

In a nonreactive saucepan, bring vinegar to a boil. Simmer and reduce until thick, like maple syrup (about 1/4 cup). Chill and reserve.

Bittersweet BISTRO

Bittersweet Bistro
Aptos
Thomas Vinolus
Chef/Proprietor

Celery Root Chips

1 large celery root

1 pint vegetable oil (canola)

Peel the celery root and slice it thinly using a mandolin or chef's knife. In a heavy pan, heat about ¹/₂ inch of oil over medium heat until it reaches 300°F, and fry the chips until they are golden brown. Remove and place on a paper towel. A pinch of salt will enhance the flavor. Figure on 3 or 4 chips per person depending on the size of the chips. You may keep these warm for a short while in the oven.

Bistro Ralph
Healdsburg
Ralph Tingle
Chef/Owner

Risotto Cakes
with Forest Mushrooms & Celery Root Chips

SERVES 6

4 cups chicken stock

1 small onion, finely chopped

10 tablespoons olive oil

2 cups Arborio rice

3 tablespoons chopped fresh thyme

¹/₂ cup grated Parmigiano-Reggiano

Salt and pepper to taste

9 tablespoons unsalted butter

1¹/₂ pounds mixed mushrooms: choose your favorite varieties from your local source or specialty market

1 tablespoon finely chopped garlic

1 tablespoon finely chopped shallot

1 tablespoon chopped parsley

Celery Root Chips (see sidebar)

1. Make the risotto first so that it will have time to cool before you cut it into cakes. In a pot, combine 3 cups of the chicken stock with 2 cups of water. Bring to a boil, reduce heat, and keep it simmering. In a second, larger pot, sauté the onions in 3 tablespoons of the olive oil. Once the onions are translucent, add the Arborio rice and stir using a wooden spoon so you don't damage the kernels. Add a few ladles of the simmering chicken stock to the rice and stir until the liquid has been absorbed. Add a few more ladles of stock and repeat this process until the rice is tender, but still has a little texture to it. This should take about 20 minutes. Add 2 tablespoons of the fresh thyme, the Parmigiano-Reggiano, and season to taste.

2. Pour the risotto into a baking dish that is large enough to make a layer of risotto about 1 inch thick. Place in the refrigerator to cool and set up. When the risotto is completely cool and firm to the touch, cut out 6 cakes. You can cut 3-inch rounds using a metal cookie cutter or cut 3-inch squares or diamonds using a knife. Heat 3 tablespoons of the olive

oil plus 1 tablespoon of the butter in a heavy sauté pan. When the oil begins to smoke, sauté the cakes over moderately high heat until golden brown on both sides. When they are finished, keep them warm in the oven while the mushrooms are cooking.

3. Cut the mushrooms into 1-inch squares or bite-size pieces. In a large sauté pan over high heat, heat 4 tablespoons of the olive oil and 4 tablespoons of the butter. Once the olive oil is smoking and the butter is melted, add the mushrooms. Stir every 2 to 3 minutes. After about 10 minutes, the mushrooms should be three-quarters cooked. Add the 1 tablespoon each of the garlic and thyme, along with the shallots and parsley. Still over high heat, add 1 cup of the chicken stock. Reduce this by half, and then add the remaining 4 tablespoons of butter, stirring or tossing to fold in the butter. Season with salt and pepper.

4. Place 1 risotto cake on each plate. Surround with mushrooms, and garnish with the celery root chips.

Chef's Recommendation: Pinot Noir, Russian River

Winter Squash Soup
with Sweet Potato Pecan Relish

SERVES 8

4 medium butternut squash, cut in half and seeded

2 sweet potatoes

1½ tablespoons extra virgin olive oil

3 large yellow onions, diced

2 carrots, peeled and coarsely chopped

1½ red bell peppers, coarsely chopped

2 jalapeño peppers, seeded and coarsely chopped

4 cloves garlic, coarsely chopped

1½ russet potatoes, peeled and cut into 2-inch cubes

Chicken stock (about 9 cups)

Kosher salt

Freshly ground black pepper

Sweet Potato Pecan Relish (see next page)

1. Preheat oven to 350°F.

2. Place squash on a lightly oiled sheet pan, cut side down. Put whole sweet potatoes on a sheet pan. Roast the squash and the potatoes in the oven until tender, approximately 1 hour. Remove from the oven, cool, and scoop the flesh from the potato and squash skins. Discard skins.

3. Heat olive oil in a large soup pot over medium heat. Add onions, carrots, red peppers, and jalapeño peppers. Sauté until onions are translucent. Add garlic and sauté for 3 more minutes, stirring often. Add sweet potato and squash, the russet potatoes, and enough chicken stock to barely cover the vegetables.

4. Bring to a boil, reduce heat, and simmer 45 minutes until potato cubes are very tender. Puree the soup in a blender and season to taste with salt and pepper. Garnish with Sweet Potato Pecan Relish.

Chef's Recommendation: Navarro Gewürztraminer Estate 1997

Boulevard
San Francisco
Nancy Oakes
Chef/Owner

Sweet Potato Pecan Relish

3 sweet potatoes, peeled and cut in 1-inch cubes

1 1/2 tablespoons rosemary

3 cloves garlic, chopped

1 red pepper, roasted, skinned, and diced

1/2 red onion, finely chopped

1/2 cup pecans, toasted and coarsely chopped

1 Anaheim chili, chopped

2 tablespoons maple syrup

1/4 cup red wine vinegar

1/2 cup olive oil

Salt and pepper, to taste

1. Preheat oven to 350°F.

2. Toss the sweet potatoes with a little olive oil, the rosemary, and the garlic. Spread on a sheet pan and roast in the oven until tender, about 1 hour. Set aside to cool.

3. Add the red pepper, red onion, pecans, and chili to the roasted sweet potatoes.

4. Combine the maple syrup, vinegar, and olive oil in a small bowl, and season to taste with salt and pepper. Toss the dressing with the vegetable mixture.

Many-Vegetable Pasta
with Feta Cheese

SERVES 4

1/3 cup extra virgin olive oil

1 medium onion, peeled and cut into small wedges

2 to 3 cloves garlic, minced medium fine

1 to 2 tablespoons chopped oregano

3 to 4 tablespoons balsamic vinegar

1/2 cup chicken or vegetable stock

3 tablespoons chopped fresh Italian parsley

Salt and freshly ground black pepper to taste

12 ounces dried pasta: angel hair and linguine work well with this recipe

4 cups cooked winter vegetables, cut into bite-size pieces. You can use any leftover roasted, steamed, or boiled winter vegetables you have on hand or choose any combination you like and follow the cooking instructions provided on the next page.

4 ounces feta cheese, crumbled slightly

Grated Parmesan cheese as a garnish

1. In a large sauté pan, heat the olive oil. Add the onions and cook until semisoft. Add the garlic, oregano, balsamic vinegar, and chicken stock. Simmer for 5 minutes. Add the parsley and season with salt and pepper.

2. Bring a large pot of water to a boil and add salt. Cook the pasta according to the directions on the package. Drain and place in a large bowl. Add the cooked winter vegetables and the onions and all their juices. Add the feta cheese and season with salt and pepper.

3. To serve, divide among four plates and garnish with grated Parmesan cheese.

Chef's Recommendation: Zinfandel

Flea Street Café
Menlo Park
Jesse Cool
Chef/Owner

Roasted Winter Vegetables: *Preheat oven to 400°F. Cut the vegetables into pieces of similar size and shape. Some good choices are carrots, parsnips, rutabagas, and potatoes. Toss the vegetables with extra virgin olive oil and place them on a baking sheet. Sprinkle with salt and pepper and roast for 20 to 30 minutes depending on the size of the vegetables. After 10 minutes turn the vegetables with a spatula and taste for tenderness.*

Steamed or Boiled Winter Vegetables: *Bring a large pot of water to a boil. If you plan to steam the vegetables, place a steamer over the pot and be sure it has a lid that fits. If you are boiling the vegetables, add a generous amount of salt to the water. Good choices for steaming and boiling are cauliflower, broccoli, kale, cabbage, and beets. Cooking times will vary according to the size and type of vegetable. It is always best to taste for doneness.*

Sautéed Winter Vegetables: *This is a great technique for cabbage and dark leafy greens such as kale and collard greens. Coat a large sauté pan with extra virgin olive oil and heat it over medium-high heat. Add the cleaned trimmed vegetables and sauté over medium-high heat until they are wilted and coated with oil. Season with salt and pepper and add ¼ inch of water. Bring to a boil and turn down the heat. Cover and simmer until the vegetable is tender.*

**Local Foods
Local Flavors**

NATIVE
Kjalii FOODS

Native Kjalii Foods, *creators of a variety of irresistible salsas and chips, believes in making fresh products from the earth's natural resources. Native Kjalii's delicious seasonal salsas are made daily from fresh produce, fresh herbs, and spices. Native Kjalii Salsas can be found in the refrigerated food section of many Bay Area supermarkets and gourmet food stores.*

This is a great year-round dish—particularly in the fall and winter, when butternut squash is in season. The cubes of roasted butternut melt into the bean broth to thicken the ragout, and the sweetness of the squash comes through nicely. It's best to roast the tomatoes in advance so they're ready when you need them. Serve with a grilled polenta, or over simple rice, or on its own with crusty hearth bread.

Winter Vegetables & White Bean Ragout

SERVES 4 TO 6

For the white beans:

$^1/_2$ cup dried cannellini or sweet white runner beans, about 3 ounces

1 quart water

2 bay leaves

1 sprig fresh marjoram or oregano

1 sprig fresh thyme

$^1/_2$ teaspoon olive oil

$^1/_4$ teaspoon salt

Freshly ground black pepper

For the ragout:

1 small butternut squash, about 1$^1/_4$ pounds, peeled and cut into $^1/_2$-inch cubes (about 3 cups)

1$^1/_2$ tablespoons light olive oil

Salt and freshly ground black pepper

1 medium yellow onion, cut into $^1/_2$-inch pieces (about 2 cups)

4 garlic cloves, finely chopped

1 medium-size red or yellow pepper, cut into thick strips, then into $^1/_2$-inch triangles (about 1$^1/_2$ cups)

2 medium-size zucchini, cut in half lengthwise and sliced into $^1/_2$-inch slices on a diagonal (about 2 cups)

$^1/_2$ teaspoon finely chopped fresh marjoram or oregano

$^1/_2$ teaspoon finely chopped fresh thyme

1 cup Roasted Tomatoes, cut in large pieces (see sidebar)

2 tablespoons finely chopped fresh parsley

15 Gaeta olives, pitted and coarsely chopped

1. Rinse, sort, and soak the beans overnight. Drain them and rinse well. Pour them into a small saucepan with the water, bay leaves, marjoram, and thyme. Bring to a boil; reduce the heat and simmer, uncovered, until tender, about 40 minutes. When the beans are completely tender yet still hold their shape, season with olive oil, salt, and a grind of black pepper. Leave the beans in their broth. Don't remove the bay leaves and sprigs of fresh herbs until you add the beans and broth to the ragout later.

Greens
San Francisco
Annie Somerville
Executive Chef

2. Preheat oven to 400°F. Toss the squash with ½ tablespoon of the olive oil and sprinkle with salt and pepper. Roast on a baking sheet until just tender, about 20 minutes.

3. Heat the remaining tablespoon of oil in a large skillet. Add the onion and ½ teaspoon salt. Sauté over medium heat until the onion is tender, about 7 to 8 minutes, adding a little water to the pan if needed. Add the garlic and peppers; sauté until the peppers are almost tender, about 10 minutes, and then add the zucchini, ¼ teaspoon salt, and a grind of black pepper. Sauté briefly to heat the zucchini through, and then add the butternut squash, the beans and their broth (remember to remove the bay leaf and herbs), and the chopped marjoram and thyme.

4. Cook, uncovered, over low heat about 15 minutes, stirring gently. Add the tomatoes and cook just long enough to heat them through, about 5 minutes, stirring gently. You should have plenty of broth in the skillet. If not, add a little water to make the ragout saucy. Add the parsley and Gaeta olives just before serving.

Chef's Recommendation: Zinfandel or wines from the southern Rhône region of France, such as Gigondas, Chateauneuf du Pape, and Vacqueyras. Look for producers such as Vieux Télégraphe, Chapoutier, and Guigal

Roasted Tomatoes

makes 1 cup

Roma (plum) tomatoes roast particularly well because their flesh is dense and they're not very juicy. This recipe requires little effort, and the full, intense flavor of the tomatoes is well worth the slow roasting time. They're a truly delicious addition to pasta, soups, stews, or cannellini beans: be sure to use every drop of their sweet juice. Since they hold well for up to a week, you may want to double the recipe and use the tomatoes for a variety of dishes.

1 pound Roma (plum) tomatoes

Extra virgin olive oil

Preheat oven to 250°F. Core the tomatoes and cut them in half crosswise. Squeeze them gently to drain their juice, and remove the seeds. Place the tomatoes cut side down on a lightly oiled baking sheet. Roast for 2 hours, until the tomatoes are very shrunken. As they slowly roast, their flesh will shrink and their skin will shrivel, but they should not brown or burn. Use immediately or refrigerate in a sealed container.

Tip: Line the baking sheet with parchment paper to keep the juice of the tomatoes from baking onto the pan. We use this technique for roasting peppers as well; it makes cleaning the pan very easy.

To prepare the tenderloin,

trim any remaining silver skin, fat, or gristle from the tenderloin and fold the tail under. Then truss the entire length to uniform thickness by tying it with cotton string at ¹/₂-inch intervals. Season with salt and coarsely ground black pepper, and sear in a hot pan to evenly brown the surface.

(continued next page)

Hawthorne Lane
San Francisco
Anne Gingrass
Executive Chef/
Proprietor

Roasted Tenderloin of Beef
with Chanterelle Bread Pudding & Warm Treviso Salad

SERVES 8

For the bread pudding:

1 tablespoon olive oil

2 tablespoons whole butter

1 pound fresh chanterelles, trimmed and sliced

Salt and pepper, to taste

6 cups cream

6 eggs

6 cups stale brioche or soft rolls, cut into ½-inch cubes

4 tablespoons fresh thyme, chopped

1 cup Pecorino cheese, grated

For the tenderloin: (see sidebar for cooking instructions)

1 four-pound whole beef tenderloin, trimmed of fat & silver skin removed

Salt and pepper to taste

¹/₂ pound fatback, sliced very thinly

For the salad:

1 cup light olive oil

2 ounces pancetta, cut into small cubes

2 cloves garlic, minced

2 shallots, minced

¹/₃ cup balsamic vinegar

2 tablespoons sherry wine vinegar

1 tablespoon whole-grain mustard

1 sprig fresh thyme

1 sprig fresh oregano

Salt and pepper to taste

2 heads frisee, blanched

2 heads radicchio di Treviso

¹/₂ cup picked Italian parsley

1. Preheat oven to 350°F.

2. To make the bread pudding, heat a sauté pan and add the oil and 1 tablespoon of the butter. Sauté the mushrooms, seasoning lightly with salt and pepper while they cook. Remove and cool. Set half aside for the salad.

3. Combine the cream and eggs in a large mixing bowl. Beat to combine, and then fold in the cubed bread, the remaining sautéed mushrooms, fresh thyme, and Pecorino. Season to taste with salt and pepper.

4. Using the remaining tablespoon of butter, butter the inside of a 10x15-inch baking dish or several smaller dishes if you would like to serve individual bread puddings like we do at the restaurant. Pour the mixture in. Place the baking dish or dishes in a roasting pan and fill the pan with enough warm water to come halfway up the side of the dish. Bake for 30 minutes. Then increase the temperature to 400°F and bake another 15 minutes or until the top becomes golden brown and a knife inserted into the center comes out clean. Reduce cooking time if using small dishes. Remove from the oven and keep warm until ready to serve.

5. Prépare the tenderloin according to the instructions in the sidebar.

6. To finish the salad, heat a sauté pan over medium heat and add about 1 tablespoon of the olive oil. Add the pancetta and sauté until crispy brown. Add the garlic and shallots—stirring well—and remove from the heat. Do not brown the garlic or shallots. Add the balsamic vinegar, sherry wine vinegar, mustard, thyme, oregano, and remaining oil. Season to taste with salt and pepper.

7. Cut the cores from the greens and wash and dry well. Tear up the frisee slightly and cut the radicchio into ½-inch slices, leaving 3-inch tips for garnish. Place the tips into one bowl, and the frisee, parsley sprigs, and chopped radicchio into another. Dress the salad and tips lightly, and arrange some of the tips around the perimeter of a serving platter with the salad in the center.

8. To finish the meat, slice the meat into ¼-inch slices and arrange 4 or 5 radicchio tips around the perimeter of another serving platter. Arrange the slices in a shingle pattern around the plate and sprinkle the reserved mushrooms around. Drizzle a small amount of vinaigrette over the meat. Serve the meat, bread puddings, and salad.

Chef's Recommendation: medium Pinot Noir

(To prepare the tenderloin continued)

Place the seared meat on a roasting rack and cover well with the fatback. Place into a 450°F oven for about 15 minutes for rare or longer to desired doneness.

(Ovens vary dramatically. It is best to use a meat thermometer to be sure. A tenderloin is usually served rare. Look for a reading of at least 120°F for very rare and 140°F for medium rare.)

Remove from the oven and allow to rest at room temperature for 10 minutes.

Empanada Stuffed with Duck Confit & Chanterelle Mushrooms

SERVES 8

4 cups flour

2 teaspoons salt

1 pound butter

²/₃ cup milk

2 tablespoons cider vinegar

2 tablespoons olive oil

2 large onions, peeled and sliced

1 tablespoon minced garlic

1 pound chanterelle mushrooms, sliced

1 tablespoon chopped parsley

1 tablespoon adobo puree or chipolte adobo (smoked jalapeños in adobo sauce), available in most Latin American grocery stores

4 cups shredded duck leg confit (available at select grocers or see recipe on page 16)

Salt and freshly ground black pepper to taste

1 egg, beaten

1. To make the dough, divide the ingredients in half and make the dough in two batches. Place the flour and salt in a food processor. Cut the butter into ¹/₂-inch chunks and add to the flour. Process until it looks like fine bread crumbs. With the machine running, add the milk and the vinegar. Process until it starts to come together. Turn it out of the processor and knead it lightly with your fingertips into a ball. Lightly flour the board. Roll each batch of dough into 10-inch circles. Place each circle on a sheet pan and refrigerate until ready to use.

2. To make the filling, heat the olive oil in a large pan. Add the onions and cook over moderate heat until they are soft and have started to caramelize. Add the garlic and the mushrooms and continue to cook until the mushrooms are soft. Add the chopped parsley, the adobo puree, and the duck confit. Mix well. Season with salt and pepper to taste. Allow to cool.

Lalime's
Berkeley
Frances Wilson
Executive Chef

3. To assemble and cook, place one of the circles of dough on a baking sheet. Pile the filling into the center of the dough and spread it out with a spatula to within 1½ inches of the edge. Brush the edges with the beaten egg. Place the other circle on top. To seal the edges, turn them over about ¾ inch and crimp them between your finger and thumb. Brush the top with beaten egg. Refrigerate for 30 minutes.

4. Preheat oven to 400°F. Bake for 10 minutes, turn down oven to 375°F, and cook for a further 35 to 45 minutes until golden brown and cooked through. Cut into slices and serve.

Chef's Recommendation: Pinot Noir, Lynmar Quail Ridge Vineyard, Russian River 1997

Celeriac & Apple Soup
with St. George Cheese Toasts

SERVES 4 TO 6

2 tablespoons sweet butter

1 large onion, peeled and chopped

3 large ribs celery, washed and chopped

4 heads of celeriac (celery root), peeled and chopped

1 large clove garlic, finely minced

2 tart apples, peeled, cored, and chopped

5 cups vegetable stock

2 cups light cream

Salt and freshly ground white pepper

1 tablespoon finely minced parsley

St. George Cheese Toasts (see sidebar)

1. Heat the butter in a soup pot; add the onion, celery, celeriac, and garlic. Sauté over medium heat for 10 minutes. Add the chopped apples and vegetable stock; bring to a boil, lower heat, and simmer uncovered for 25 minutes or until the vegetables are soft.

2. Puree the soup in a food processor until smooth and return to the pot. Add the cream slowly while stirring gently. Bring to the boiling point, but do not boil. Season with salt and pepper to taste. Sprinkle with parsley. Serve hot, accompanied by St. George Cheese Toasts.

St. George Cheese Toasts

4 to 6 slices of crusty French bread

Virgin olive oil

4 ounces St. George cheese (Mattos Cheese Company) or Gruyère, grated

Heat the broiler. Brush the bread slices with olive oil, and toast in the broiler until golden brown. Cover each toasted slice with cheese and return to the broiler until the cheese melts.

Coriander-Cured Lamb
with Dried Cherry-Zinfandel Sauce & Basil Mashed Potatoes

SERVES 6

6 tablespoons coriander seeds

6 tablespoons black peppercorns

6 shallots, minced

6 large garlic cloves, minced

1/2 cup kosher (coarse) salt

9 tablespoons dark-brown sugar

1/2 cup virgin olive oil

6 six-ounce lamb top sirloin (boneless lamb) cutlets

3 tablespoons vegetable oil

Dried Cherry-Zinfandel Sauce (see next page)

Basil Mashed Potatoes (see next page)

1. Place the coriander and peppercorns in the bowl of a food processor and process for about 1 minute until coarsely ground. Add the shallots, garlic, salt, and sugar. With the machine running, drizzle in the olive oil to make a thick paste. Transfer to an 8-inch-square glass pan and add the lamb to cure for at least 3 hours, turning occasionally. Note: If you are sensitive to the volatile oils in onions, transferring the paste to the glass pan may make your eyes sting.

2. Preheat oven to 400°F.

3. Heat the vegetable oil in a hot, heavy skillet over medium heat until lightly smoking. Remove the lamb from the cure and scrape clean. Season with additional salt to taste and sear on all sides in the skillet. Transfer to an ovenproof baking dish and cook in the oven for 15 to 18 minutes for medium rare. The lamb will continue to cook after it is removed from the oven, so be careful not to overcook. When the lamb is done, remove from the oven and let rest 3 to 5 minutes.

4. Slice the lamb and arrange on top of the Dried Cherry-Zinfandel Sauce. Serve with Basil Mashed Potatoes.

Chef's Recommendation: Zinfandel, Turley Grist Vineyard, Dry Creek 1997

Cafe Lolo
Santa Rosa
Michael Quigley
Chef/Owner

Dried Cherry-Zinfandel Sauce

1 tablespoon virgin olive oil

1/2 pound wild mushrooms, sliced

2 cups Zinfandel

1/4 cup sugar

3 tablespoons red wine vinegar

1 quart veal or beef stock

1 cup dried cherries

Salt and freshly ground black pepper to taste

1. Heat the olive oil in a hot sauté pan over medium heat. Add the mushrooms and sauté until soft. Remove from heat and set aside.

2. Combine Zinfandel, sugar, and vinegar in a saucepan over medium heat and, stirring occasionally, reduce to 1/2 cup. Add the veal stock and simmer until reduced by one-third, approximately 15 minutes. Add the cherries and simmer another 10 minutes. Season with salt and pepper to taste. Add the sautéed mushrooms and simmer 2 more minutes. Keep hot.

Basil Mashed Potatoes

10 medium potatoes, peeled and quartered

2 tablespoons sweet butter, softened

1 cup whole milk

1 bunch basil, washed and trimmed

1/2 cup virgin olive oil

Salt and freshly ground white pepper to taste

1. Place the quartered potatoes in a large pot and cover with water by 2 inches. Bring to a boil, reduce heat, and simmer until done. Drain; add the butter and half the milk. Mash to desired consistency, adding milk as necessary.

2. Blanch basil in boiling water for 5 seconds and drop immediately into ice water. Squeeze basil completely dry in a towel or two. Coarsely chop basil and place in blender. Turn blender on and slowly add the olive oil. Mix this basil puree into mashed potatoes until incorporated. Add salt and pepper to taste.

CELEBRATING THE BASICS OF

GOOD FARMING AND THE FUNDAMENTALS

OF SUSTAINABLE AGRICULTURE

BAY AREA SPRING CROPS

APRICOTS	MORELS
ARTICHOKES	MUSTARD GREENS
ARUGULA	NASTURTIUMS
ASPARAGUS	NEW POTATOES
BEETS	ONIONS
BLACKBERRIES	PATTYPAN SQUASH
BLOOD ORANGES	PEA SHOOTS
BLUEBERRIES	RADISHES
BOYSENBERRIES	RASPBERRIES
CARROTS	RHUBARB
CEPES	SALAD GREENS
CHANTERELLES	SNAP PEAS
CHARD	SNOW PEAS
CHERRIES	SORREL
ENGLISH PEAS	SPINACH
ESCAROLE	SPRING ONIONS
FAVA BEANS	STRAWBERRIES
FENNEL	TURNIPS
FRISEE	WATERCRESS
GREEN BEANS	ZUCCHINI
GREEN GARLIC	
LEEKS	
MEYER LEMONS	

The season springs forth its hope
A plum's black wood gives bloom of purest white
Each blossom resonates resurrection's theme
Every tree, bush, and weed sends up a bee's delight.

Like the bee, we hurry to our tasks
The earth awakens to the cold edge of steel
No day's labor completed, no repose by night
Will the beauty of the expectant seed be revealed?

Earthly remains of growth once flourishing
Consumed, decayed, rotting detail abound
Unless a grain of wheat dies, it has no being
In this fragrant mould, abundant promise is found.

Silty, sandy, muddy Earth
We savor God's ardent endowment in you!
Make us worthy stewards of your robust gifts
In wonderment and fright we witness life renew.

—Denesse Willey '98

Here in the fruited plain of California's Great Central Valley, the early inklings of spring start in February. The vegetables we have been harvesting through the winter—turnips, arugula, spinach, beets, lettuce, and the like—will be going to seed. It's sap-risin' time, as ole Mr. Poe used to say. The buds on fruit trees will swell. By the end of the month, white, pink, and lavender blossoms will burst open on thousands of acres of orchards. Honeybees from all over the United States are brought into the Central Valley area "to serve its beauty right," as Robert Frost said.

The Farm Life

T&D WILLEY FARMS

Certified organic since 1987, T&D Willey Farms is located on 75 acres in the geographic center of the Great Central Valley of California. Growing everything from arugula to rutabagas, T&D Willey Farms employs 25 people full-time year-round. The hallmark of its produce is high-quality packaging, which means paper-lined wooden boxes, each including a public information document.

Truckloads of compost are delivered to our farm. We will look for a break in the rains so we can spread the soil food that nourishes nature's fertility factory: soil microbes. Healthy plants stave off disease and insect pressure. Healthy plants start with healthy soil.

For the farmer, spring is a time of both intense anxiety and eager anticipation. A titanic volume of work looms ahead and grows with the lengthening days: ground work, transplanting, trellising, seeding, cultivating a dozen different crops. Forgotten tasks, or the fear of them, creep into our dreams. Yet, great hope is poured over our frantic attempts. Each year we are given the chance to benefit from previous mistakes. We're excited to see what our new ideas and experimental plantings will reveal. And, of course, there is baseball. Little League tryouts start in February followed by almost daily practice in March. Then two games a week for 10 weeks for two school-age boys.

By the time the weather turns hot, it will be near the end of the school year. Three-quarters of our farm will be planted. Miles of drip tape will have been laid out, and irrigation will be a daily chore occupying two or three men. Thousands of stakes will be used to tie up either peas—at the end of their harvest—or tomatoes—at their peak production—or eggplant, and the work will begin in earnest once the temperature is consistently above 90 degrees. The Little League season will be over and the pennant races shaping up in the big leagues. Spring will be over, and we will be starting to prepare our open ground for winter vegetables.

by Denesse Willey
T&D Willey Farms
Madera, California

What Is Organic?

The heart of organic agriculture is in caring for the soil. Organic farmers and gardeners nurture soil by adding composts, turning under cover crops and natural fertilizers, avoiding excessive tillage, and shunning synthetic substances that damage or disturb the balance of living soil. Good tilth—a diversity of visible and microscopic insects, fungi, and bacteria—adequate water retention, well-balanced minerals, and a rich store of organic matter are indicators of healthy soil.

The vast majority of organic farms are small operations. Unlike industrialized conventional farms, organic farms tend to grow a variety of crops and many of them integrate plant and livestock production. Relying as they do on natural forces, organic farmers are less likely to grow crops in regions or climates that are poorly suited to those crops—therefore requiring high levels of fertilization, pesticides, or other inputs.

Around the world, organic producers share a common set of principles. Most basic is their attitude toward nature; they seek to understand and cooperate with natural forces and cycles rather than dominate them. Organic methods of production—rotating crops, relying on natural balances and cycles, using varieties of crops that are resistant to diseases and pests, careful timing, fertilizing only with natural materials—stem from the desire to work with nature.

In the marketplace, retailers—eager to summarize the essence of organic foods in easy-to-grasp sound bites—use negative expressions, such as *no pesticides, no fertilizers,* and *no antibiotics.* The terms are misleading because organic producers do use pesticides and fertilizers, but only those made of natural materials. Some organic growers control pests and diseases with rotenone, ryania, sabadilla, pyrethrums, sulfur, and copper. Most organic growers fertilize with composts, manures, and mined-rock powders. While rejecting feed that contains antibiotics and hormones, many organic livestock farmers use antibiotics to treat animals that are sick.

Knowing your farmer is the best assurance that the food you buy is organically grown. If you can't buy from a farmer you know personally, then verify that a respected organic certification program has certified the food as organic. There are many organic certifiers in the United States; some of the programs are private, and others are run by state departments of agriculture.

Any system of certification or accreditation is only as good as the integrity of the producers of the food. Organic agriculture is possible as a purely technical approach to producing food. However, organic farming and processing are most reliable when they follow from the philosophical

by Elizabeth Henderson

conviction of the producers. Organic farmers and processors understand that everything in this world is connected to everything else. They seek to work in harmony with natural forces and to leave in better condition than when they found it that little piece of the world over which they have stewardship.

Can We Have an Organic Food System?

Despite the agronomic and commercial successes of organic farming, policy shapers and makers still dismiss the potential for wholesale conversion to organic methods. The arguments against conversion are clothed as sober, scientific assessments when in fact they are flagrantly unscientific. Can the organic farming model match the productivity and reliability of today's chemical-intensive model? It's impossible to say, because the scientific effort to understand and optimize organic farming has never been seriously applied. The Organic Farming Research Foundation (OFRF) has documented the near-total absence of government research devoted to organic systems. Out of roughly $1.8 billion in federal funding for agricultural research and extension in 1995, less than 1/10 of 1 percent was spent investigating organic farming. Out of 30,000 projects in the research database of the U.S. Department of Agriculture, the OFRF found only 34 it could identify as focused explicitly on organic systems.

For the past 50 years, organic farming has been essentially taboo within the agricultural research system. All of the success achieved by organic farmers has come with almost no support—and often with outright hostility—from university and government researchers. In many ways, the art and science of organic agriculture are still in their infancy. There is vast potential for improving and optimizing organic management.

Attitudes about organic research are finally starting to change. Backed by massive grassroots political support, the federal government has begun to allocate resources to organic farming research and education. Universities are dedicating research ground to organic management and creating faculty appointments. Many challenges lie ahead in guiding and nurturing those investments, but it is a scientific frontier of the first importance.

by Mark Lipson
Policy Program
Director
Organic Farming
Research
Foundation

Regional Family Farms

The **Organic Farming Research Foundation** sponsors research related to organic farming practices, disseminates research results to organic farmers and to growers interested in adopting organic production systems, and educates both the public and decision makers about organic farming issues. Founded in 1990, it is the only organization in the United States that supports organic farming grant-making research and advocacy. Its board of directors is composed of organic farmers, researchers, and activists from around the nation.

Eating fresh, nutritious food has become harder and harder to do for the past few generations. It's not just because of fast-food restaurants or the explosion of junk food manufacturers. Nor is it simply the overuse of pesticides on our crops and the antibiotics force-fed to our animals. When it comes to growing fresh, nutritious food, our biggest concern is the soil in which it is grown or raised. We must stop treating our soil like dirt.

Most nutritionists today agree we are not getting enough minerals in our diets. We hear about calcium, iron, and potassium deficiencies as the culprits causing a host of disease-related symptoms. Those minerals are critical building blocks for numerous enzymatic and amino acid reactions in our bodies, as well as in a number of other biophysical and biochemical processes. How do we get important minerals into our diets? By taking vitamin pills? Drinking supershakes? Not quite. The minerals our bodies need should come from the foods we eat. Too often, though, those foods suffer from the same nutritional deficiencies. Even the fresh foods we assume are mineral rich—and compared with our local fast-food menus, they are—suffer from deficiencies because of the soil in which they are grown.

Good Health Starts with Good Soil

What is the difference between soil and dirt?

According to Webster, dirt is defined as "excrement, something worthless, a filthy or soiling substance." It's interesting how the word soil sneaks into the definition of dirt. Soil, on the other hand, is described as "any substance or medium in which something may take root or grow, disintegrated rock with an admixture of organic matter and soluble salts (humus)." The truth is, soil is a dynamic, living environment made up of mineral and organic constituents. It is home to tens of thousands, if not hundreds of thousands, of different species of microbial organisms. Those organisms provide nutrients for plants and build organic matter in the soil. As their populations diminish, so does the nutrient value of our foods.

Today's organic farmers—and even many conventional farmers—are starting to realize that healthy food starts with healthy soil. And in order to maintain healthy soil, we must create sustainable soil and crop management systems. Good soil management focuses on balancing the chemical, biological, and physical structure of the soil as one entity. This becomes a building-block process. Without balanced-soil chemistry, soil's physical structure restricts air and water flow, which in turn shuts down soil biology. It is that biology that drives most of the activity in the soil and that ultimately becomes responsible for nutrient mobility. The soil

by Joel Simmons
EarthWorks
Natural Organic
Products
Martins Creek,
Pennsylvania

microbes that make up such a dynamic biological environment need food in the same fashion that we do, and for the most part their food comes from the carbohydrates found in soil humus. When we overuse synthetic, high-salt fertilizers, organic matter gets burned out of the soil, and food reserves for microbes are reduced. This limits their activity—thereby affecting the overall balance of the soil—and restricts mineral availability to the plant and, therefore, to all of us. It also puts stress on the plant, which weakens the plant and creates an environment for insect and disease attack. That leads to the use of pesticides, which further destroys microbial populations and thus causes the beginning of an endless cycle.

As consumers, we are much more concerned about clean food than ever before, but there is more to it than just being free of pesticides. From a soil science standpoint, pesticides are not the real problem. The real problem is poor and imbalanced soil that creates the stress on the plant and that generates the need for the pesticides. The better growers of organic foods not only are providing their customers with clean food; most likely, they are also providing consumers with food that is rich in minerals through good soil management. That is why you can taste the difference in most organic foods. The relationship between human health and healthy soil is amazing. If we can get our food from healthy soils, there is no question that we can build and maintain our own sustainable health.

Resources for Living Local

Chefs Collaborative 2000 (CC2000) is a growing network of over 1,500 of America's most influential and well-known chefs, who work collectively to advance sustainable food choices for the next century. Founded in 1993 by chefs as an educational initiative of Oldways Preservation & Exchange Trust, the collaborative is committed to developing educational programs for children, to strengthening farmer-chef connections, and to providing good, safe, and wholesome food by emphasizing locally grown, seasonally fresh, and whole or minimally processed food in their restaurants. Local chapters exist throughout the Bay Area.

We as consumers can make food choices that not only enhance our own health but also contribute to the protection of our natural resources and the long-term sustainability of the food system. The following guidelines can help you in planning your family's diet and making healthier, greener food choices.

8 Simple Steps to the New Green Diet

1. Eat a variety of food.

When you eat a wide variety of food, a broad range of nutritional requirements is likely to be met. You also draw on biological diversity. The proliferating "variety" in supermarkets does not reflect biological variety, since so many of the hundreds of available products are made from the same relatively few raw food materials—corn, wheat, rice, and potatoes. People today rely on just 20 varieties of plants for 90 percent of their food. Instead, you can eat a wider variety of whole foods instead of food novelties, whose claims to diversity are based on processing techniques and artificial colors and flavors.

2. Buy locally produced food.

The average mouthful of food travels 1,200 miles from farm to factory to warehouse to supermarket to our plates. In comparison, food available from local farms is almost always fresher, tastier and closer to ripeness. In addition, buying local products supports regional growers, thereby preserving farming near where you live and requiring less energy for transport. Since the production of a wide variety of fruits and vegetables is more economical if the farmers have outlets for their produce nearby, local marketing should be encouraged. And because it isn't being shipped long distances, local food is less likely to have been treated with post-harvest pesticides.

3. Buy produce in season.

Out-of-season produce is extravagant because it is so amazingly energy intensive. It costs about 435 calories to fly one 5-calorie strawberry from California to New York. Out-of-season produce is also more likely to have been imported, possibly from a country with less stringent pesticide regulations than the U.S. Eating frozen fruits and vegetables, especially from local producers, is your very best option during the winter months. Frozen foods retain much of their nutritional content, in addition to cutting energy costs.

*Mothers &
Others
from The Green
Food Shopper*

4. Buy organically produced food.

Organically grown means that the food has been grown in a practical, ecological partnership with nature. To maintain its integrity, organic food is minimally processed and is without artificial ingredients, preservatives, or irradiation. Organic certification is the public's guarantee that the product has been grown and handled according to strict procedures without synthetic chemical inputs.

5. Eat fresh, whole foods with adequate starch and fiber.

Whole foods—including fruits, vegetables, grains, legumes (beans), nuts, and seeds—are the healthiest foods we can eat. The National Cancer Institute recommends we each "strive for five" servings of fresh fruits and vegetables a day, since the complex carbohydrates and fiber they contain play a major beneficial role in protecting against cancer, heart disease, and common digestive ailments.

6. Eat fewer and smaller portions of animal products.

Modern meat production involves intensive use of grain, water, energy, and grazing areas. It takes about 390 gallons of water to produce a pound of beef. Almost half of the energy used in American agriculture goes into livestock production. Cattle and other livestock consume more than 70 percent of the grain produced in the U.S. and about a third of the world's total grain harvest. Animal agriculture also produces surprisingly large amounts of air and water pollution. Pork is the most resource intensive, followed by beef, then poultry. Eggs and dairy products are much less resource intensive. Animal products, especially beef, are also a major source of fat in the U.S. diet. Reducing meat consumption and eating lower on the food chain protects us against heart disease, cancer, and diabetes.

7. Choose minimally processed and packaged foods.

After it leaves the farm, food is subjected to a variety of processes (including packaging), most of which use fossil energy while removing naturally occurring nutrients. A typical highly processed (and highly advertised) "food product" may contain on average only 7 percent real food. Processing provides no value for the biological variety of the diet when the refined-food fraction is converted into hundreds of products high in fat, salt, or sugar.

8. Prepare your own meals at home.

Cooking from scratch can involve a little more labor and a little more time, but you can be sure you'll save money and resources, because you're not paying someone else to prepare your food, to add nutrients removed in processing, to put it in a box or can, to ship it across the country, and to advertise it in slick TV commercials. You will also provide your family with healthier, more nutritious food, since you are starting with fresh ingredients. And, cooking from scratch can be its own reward, providing a truly creative outlet that brings us pleasure and joy, rejuvenates the family meal, and nourishes our bodies and our souls.

Parts of these Eight Steps are adapted from Joan Dye Gussow and Katherine L. Clancy, "Dietary Guidelines for Sustainability," Journal of Nutrition Education, Vol.18, No.1, 1986.

Resources for Living Local

For A Livable Planet

Mothers & Others is a national nonprofit education organization that promotes consumer choices that are safe and ecologically sustainable. Formed in 1989 based on concern that children were being exposed to unsafe pesticide levels in food, the organization has gone on to tackle many other environmental issues that affect the health of women and children. Among its many projects, Mothers & Others has done exceptional work with its Shoppers' Campaign for Healthy Food, Farms & Families, organizing consumers to vote with their dollars in support of farmers who are utilizing safer, more sustainable production methods. The Shoppers' Campaign Toolbox contains a wealth of information—including the 10 Most Important Foods to Buy Organic, 8 Simple Steps to the New Green Diet, Information on Community-Supported Agriculture, Information on Food Cooperatives, Shopping for Organic Fact Sheet, What Is Integrated Pest Management (IPM)? and What Are Ecolabels?— all of which can be found on the Mothers & Others Web site at http://www.mothers.org.

GRILLED ASPARAGUS WITH MEYER LEMON VINAIGRETTE
& SHAVED BELLWETHER PECORINO PEPATO
  Annie Somerville, Greens 58

SPRING VEGETABLE & LEMONGRASS STEW WITH POACHED GROUPER
  George Cronk, Park Grill 59

FRISEE & ARUGULA SALAD WITH SPRING CHANTERELLES, GREEN GARLIC & CROUTONS
  Wendy Brucker, Rivoli 60

ROASTED CHICKEN WITH TARRAGON PEACH SAUCE
  Jesse Cool, Flea Street Café 61

ARTICHOKE TORTA (FRITTATA)
  Paul Bertolli, Oliveto 62

CRAB & ASPARAGUS SOUP WITH GREEN ONIONS & CILANTRO
  Anne Gingrass, Hawthorne Lane 64

GRILLED DAY BOAT SCALLOPS
  Michael Quigley, Cafe Lolo 66

ASPARAGUS WITH BALSAMIC SYRUP & PARMIGIANO-REGGIANO
  Ralph Tingle, Bistro Ralph 67

SHAVED RAW ARTICHOKES, FAVA BEANS & PARMESAN
  Reed Hearon, Rose Pistola 68

SOUTHWESTERN ASPARAGUS, CORN & TOMATILLO SOUP
  Eric Tucker, Millennium 69

SPRING VEGETABLE SOUP
  Bradley Ogden, Lark Creek Inn 70

PROVENÇAL VEGETABLE RAGOUT
  Jody Denton, Restaurant LuLu 72

ASPARAGUS & BUTTERMILK SOUP
  David Kinch, Restaurant Sent Sovi 73

GLAZED OYSTERS WITH LEEK FONDUE
  Gary Danko, Gary Danko 74

FEUILLETÉE OF MORELS, ARTICHOKES, ROASTED FENNEL & FAVA BEANS
WITH AN ASPARAGUS BEURRE BLANC
  Frances Wilson, Lalime's 76

STRAWBERRY SOUP WITH LEMON BALM GRANITA
  Judith Maguire, Lalime's 78

ASPARAGUS SALAD WITH MEYER LEMON VINAIGRETTE
  Thomas Vinolus, Bittersweet Bistro 79

ALMOND TART WITH FRESH BERRIES & FRESH STRAWBERRY ICE CREAM
  Kathleen Berman, Mixx 80

SPRING LAMB CHOPS WITH FAVA-MASHED POTATOES
  Judy Rodgers, Zuni 82

JUST-BAKED WILD BOYSENBERRY SHORTCAKE
  Nancy Oakes, Boulevard 83

RAGOUT OF SPRING VEGETABLES WITH AGED SHERRY VINEGAR & GREEN OLIVE OIL
  Daniel Patterson, Elisabeth Daniel 84

Spring
Recipes

Grilled Asparagus with Meyer Lemon Vinaigrette & Shaved Bellwether Pecorino Pepato

SERVES 4

1 pound thick asparagus spears, woody ends removed

Light olive oil

Salt and freshly ground pepper

1 bunch watercress

Meyer Lemon Vinaigrette (see below)

1 small wedge Bellwether Pecorino Pepato cheese

1. Prepare the charcoal grill.

2. Parboil the asparagus in lightly salted water for a minute or 2, until just tender. Drain and run under cool water. Brush the asparagus lightly with olive oil and sprinkle with salt and pepper. Grill over a medium-hot fire for about 5 minutes, turning the asparagus until the skin is slightly charred and the spears tender.

3. Wash the watercress, dry it in a spinner, and arrange it on a platter. Place the grilled asparagus on the watercress; drizzle with vinaigrette. Using a vegetable peeler, shave the Pecorino Pepato over the asparagus and serve.

Chef's Recommendation: Alsatian Riesling or Gewürztraminer. Look for wines from Zind Humbrecht, Leon Beyer, or Roland Schmidt. Another option would be a big, rich Chardonnay like those from Kistler, Forman, or Kalin.

Meyer Lemon Vinaigrette

makes about ¹/₂ cup

Zest of 1 Meyer lemon, minced

2 tablespoons fresh Meyer lemon juice

1 tablespoon champagne vinegar

¹/₂ teaspoon salt

¹/₈ teaspoon freshly ground black pepper

6 tablespoons light olive oil

Combine everything but the oil in a small bowl. Then drizzle the oil in and whisk. Whisk in a little mustard if you're using ordinary lemons.

Greens
San Francisco
Annie Somerville
Executive Chef

Spring Vegetable & Lemongrass Stew
with Poached Grouper

SERVES 4

4 cups chicken stock

Salt and pepper to taste

2 stalks lemongrass, peeled, sliced thin, and chopped fine

$\frac{1}{2}$ teaspoon chopped garlic

2 artichokes, peeled, cooked, and chopped

$\frac{1}{2}$ fennel, julienned

4 seven-ounce portions of grouper

$\frac{1}{8}$ cup blanched and shucked fava beans

$\frac{1}{2}$ teaspoon soy sauce

Juice of $\frac{1}{2}$ lemon

1 Roma tomato, peeled, seeded, and diced

4 large basil leaves, roughly chopped

1 teaspoon butter

4 basil sprigs, for garnish

1. Bring the chicken stock to a boil and reduce by half. Turn down the heat and season with salt and pepper to taste. Add the lemongrass and garlic. Cover and let simmer for about 15 to 20 minutes. Strain the stock.

2. Add artichokes and fennel to the strained stock and cook until tender. Remove the artichokes and fennel and set aside.

3. Place the grouper in the simmering liquid and cook until done, about 5 minutes. Remove the fish and place it in a bowl.

4. To the simmering liquid, add the shucked fava beans, soy sauce, lemon juice, Roma tomato, artichoke/fennel mix, basil, and butter. Heat until warmed. Check seasoning and ladle the liquid over the fish. Garnish with basil sprig.

Chef's Recommendation: Sauvignon Blanc, Cakebread 1997

⊞ PARK GRILL ⊞

Park Hyatt
San Francisco
San Francisco
George Cronk
Former Executive
Chef

Frisee & Arugula Salad
with Spring Chanterelles, Green Garlic & Croutons

SERVES 6

$^1/_2$ pound chanterelles, thinly sliced

2 green garlic bulbs and leaves, finely chopped

$^1/_2$ cup plus 1 teaspoon virgin olive oil

1 teaspoon fresh thyme, chopped

Salt and freshly ground black pepper

1 cup cubed sourdough bread, with crust if desired

3 tablespoons red wine vinegar

1 teaspoon Dijon mustard

4 scant handfuls frisee

4 scant handfuls arugula

1 scant handful stemmed Italian flat-leaf parsley, leaves left whole

$^1/_3$ cup shaved Pecorino

1. Sauté mushrooms and green garlic over high heat with 2 tablespoons of the olive oil. When the liquid has almost completely cooked off, toss with thyme, and salt and pepper to taste. Remove from heat and set aside.

2. Preheat oven to 425°F. To make the croutons, toss the sourdough bread cubes with 1 tablespoon of the olive oil. Place, in one layer, on a cookie sheet, and toast in oven until lightly browned, about 5 to 8 minutes.

3. Prepare the vinaigrette by whisking together the remaining $^1/_3$ cup of olive oil, red wine vinegar, mustard, and salt and pepper to taste.

4. Toss together frisee, arugula, prepared mushrooms and croutons, parsley, and vinaigrette to lightly coat greens. Divide among 6 plates and sprinkle with shaved Pecorino.

Chef's Recommendation: Riesling

Rivoli

Rivoli
Berkeley
Wendy Brucker
Chef/Owner

Roasted Chicken
with Tarragon Peach Sauce

SERVES 4

1 three-and-one-half-pound chicken

Olive oil, salt, and pepper to season the chicken

2 medium leeks, white and light-green parts only, thoroughly washed and sliced thin

3 medium peaches, peeled, pitted, and sliced

1/2 teaspoon grated nutmeg

1 teaspoon ground cinnamon

2 tablespoons chopped fresh tarragon

3 tablespoons brown sugar

1. Preheat oven to 400°F.

2. Remove the liver, neck, and giblet package from the chicken. Pull away the flaps of fat from the opening of the cavity and rinse the chicken inside and out. Pat it dry with paper towels. Rub the outside with olive oil, and season generously with salt and pepper. Place in a deep roasting pan.

3. In a bowl, combine the leeks, peaches, nutmeg, cinnamon, tarragon, and brown sugar. Spoon the mixture around the bottom of the chicken in the pan. Roast the chicken in the oven for 30 minutes at 400°F. Then reduce the heat to 375°F and continue cooking until the chicken is done, about 55 minutes. To check for doneness, either pierce at the joint of the thigh and the breast to see if the juices run clear, or insert an instant-read thermometer into the breast. It should read 155°F to 160°F. While the chicken is roasting, stir the peach/leek mixture occasionally to keep it from burning.

4. Remove the chicken from the oven and place it on a platter, cover it with foil, and allow it to rest for 15 to 20 minutes. Cut the chicken into pieces and serve it with the leeks, peaches, and pan juices over steamed rice.

Chef's Recommendation: Riesling or Chardonnay

Flea Street Café
Menlo Park
Jesse Cool
Chef/Owner

I like to use small artichokes about the size of a golf ball; they are very tender (small artichokes such as these have no chokes) and flavorful and make for an appealing visual effect when the frittata is cross sectioned. If small ones are not available, larger chokes may be used. It will be necessary to pare them down to their bottoms, remove the choke with the sharp edge of a spoon, and cut the artichoke bottoms into pieces prior to cooking them.

Oliveto
Oakland
Paul Bertolli
Chef/Owner

Artichoke Torta (Frittata)

SERVES 8 TO 10 AS AN APPETIZER

8 whole eggs

$^1/_2$ cup half-and-half

$^1/_2$ teaspoon salt

$^1/_4$ teaspoon finely ground black pepper

$^3/_4$ cup grated creamy Havarti cheese (also called Dofino)

$^1/_2$ cup grated Reggiano Parmigiano

1 bunch spinach, cleaned and stemmed

1 bunch fresh basil, chopped coarsely

2 ounces Prosciutto di Parma, sliced thin, then cut into small dice

12 small spring artichokes or 5 or 6 globe artichokes

$2^1/_2$ tablespoons olive oil

2 shallots, minced

Juice of $^1/_4$ lemon

$^1/_3$ cup water

1. Preheat oven to 375°F.

2. In a large bowl, crack the eggs and beat slightly. Pour in the half-and-half, salt, and pepper. Add the Havarti cheese and the Reggiano Parmigiano.

3. Bring a pot of water to a boil. Plunge in the spinach and cook for 2 minutes. Drain the spinach in a colander and refresh it under cold water. Using your hands, squeeze out as much water as possible from the spinach. Transfer it to a cutting board and chop fine. Add the chopped spinach, basil, and Prosciutto di Parma to the egg mixture. Stir to mix well. Set aside.

4. If you are using larger chokes, pare the artichokes down to their tender centers or bottoms and cut them in half. Warm 1 tablespoon of the olive oil in a seasoned small skillet or a 6-inch nonstick pan. Add the shallots and cook them over medium heat for 2 minutes. Add the artichokes,

lemon juice, and water. Sprinkle over a little salt and cover the pan. Cook the artichokes for about 10 minutes or until tender in the center when pierced with the point of a knife. Remove the cover and, keeping the artichokes in the pan, reduce away any liquid remaining in the pan. Let cool briefly, add the shallots and artichokes to the egg mixture, and stir well.

5. Create a water bath by choosing a baking dish that is large enough to hold the small skillet or 6-inch pan and filling it with warm water to about a quarter of the skillet/pan's depth. Place the water bath aside.

6. Place the remaining 1½ tablespoons of olive oil into the skillet or pan and warm it until a drop of the egg mixture sputters. Add the egg mixture to the pan and cook for 4 to 5 minutes. Using the edge of a spatula, lift the torta away from the edges of the pan to gauge its progress. When you see that the torta has browned nicely all around, remove it from the heat and immediately place the pan into the water bath to stop the browning (this will cause a lot of steam and some splattering). Carefully place the torta and water bath in the oven and bake for 50 to 55 minutes or until the torta is firm in the center and brown on top.

7. Turn out the torta, bottom side up, onto a cutting board and cut into 1-inch chunks. Serve the torta pieces, top side up, at room temperature.

Chef's Recommendation: Vernaccia, Terre di Tufi Teruzzi e Puthod 1996 or a simple crisp white wine or rosé

Crab & Asparagus Soup
with Green Onions and Cilantro

SERVES 4

½ cup shallots, peeled and sliced into thin rings

2 tablespoons peanut oil

8 ounces picked Dungeness crabmeat

1 pound asparagus, thick ends removed and cut into ⅛-inch rounds

4 cups low-sodium chicken stock

2 eggs, beaten

1 tablespoon cornstarch

1 tablespoon water

3 tablespoons soy sauce

2 tablespoons Thai fish sauce

White pepper, to taste

3 tablespoons chopped cilantro

3 tablespoons chopped green onions, green part only

1 cup pea sprouts, available at Asian markets

Tempura-Fried Asparagus Spears, for garnish (see next page)

1. Sweat the shallots in the oil over medium heat until translucent. Add the crabmeat and asparagus and sauté for 2 minutes, stirring gently so as not to shred the meat.

2. Add the chicken stock and bring to a boil. Slowly pour the eggs in while stirring gently.

3. Combine the cornstarch and water in a small bowl and mix thoroughly to make a slurry. Pour into the boiling soup while stirring, and cook for 5 minutes.

4. Remove from the heat and add the soy sauce, fish sauce, and white pepper.

5. Ladle into warm, deep bowls and garnish with the cilantro, green onions, pea sprouts, and Tempura-Fried Asparagus Spears. Serve immediately.

Chef's Recommendation: spicy French Gewürztraminer

**Hawthorne
Lane**
San Francisco
Anne Gingrass
Executive Chef/
Proprietor

Tempura-Fried Asparagus Spears

recipe by Martha Hester Stafford

4 asparagus stalks, tough ends discarded

Vegetable oil for frying

1 egg yolk

1 cup ice water

1 cup sifted flour

$^1/_2$ cup extra flour for dredging

Slice the asparagus into $^1/_2$-inch diagonal pieces. Heat at least 3 inches of oil in a deep, heavy saucepan to 350°F. Prepare the batter just before you are ready to fry. When the oil is hot, beat the egg yolk in a small bowl. Add water and beat a few times. Dump the flour in all at once and stir only 3 or 4 times. The batter should be very lumpy. Test the oil by dropping a few drops of batter in it. The drops should sink all the way to the bottom and rise up right away. Put the dredging flour on a plate. Dry the asparagus and dip them in the flour. Shake off the excess flour and dip them in the batter. In the oil, place a few pieces at a time and fry until golden brown. Drain on paper towel.

*3 egg yolks (see
note on page 175)*

Juice of 1 lemon

*1 clove garlic,
chopped*

*2 bunches
tarragon, chopped*

1 1/2 cup olive oil

1/2 cup buttermilk

*Salt and pepper
to taste*

*Place the egg
yolks, lemon
juice, garlic, and
tarragon in the
bowl of a food
processor, and
buzz for 30
seconds. Then,
with the machine
running, slowly
add oil, butter-
milk, and salt
and pepper. If the
dressing is too
thick, add a little
more buttermilk.*

Grilled Day Boat Scallops

SERVES 3 AS MAIN COURSE OR 6 AS APPETIZER

3/4 cup pearl onions, peeled

1 teaspoon olive oil

3/4 cup fresh peas, shelled and blanched in boiling salted water

3/4 cup fresh corn kernels, blanched in boiling salted water

3/4 cup diced fennel

3/4 cup chopped Applewood smoked bacon, cooked

Salt and pepper, to taste

Creamy Tarragon Dressing (see sidebar)

18 fresh sea scallops

6 sprigs Italian parsley

1. Preheat oven to 400°F.

2. Toss the peeled onions in olive oil. Place in a small pan and roast in the oven for 20 minutes, stirring occasionally.

3. In a bowl, toss together peas, corn, pearl onions, fennel, and bacon. Add salt and pepper and 3/4 cup of the Creamy Tarragon Dressing and let stand.

4. Prepare a grill, or heat a grill pan on the stove. Season scallops with salt and pepper. Grill on a hot grill until cooked through, about 2 minutes on each side. Remove from heat.

5. Place a neat pile of the vegetable mixture in the center of the plate. Divide the scallops evenly among the plates, placing them around the vegetable mixture. Drizzle a small amount of the Creamy Tarragon Dressing over the scallops, garnish with Italian parsley, and serve.

Chef's Recommendation: Chardonnay, Flowers Camp Meeting Ridge 1997

C A F E

Lolo

Cafe Lolo
Santa Rosa
Michael Quigley
Chef/Owner

Asparagus with Balsamic Syrup
& Parmigiano-Reggiano

SERVES 6

2 pounds large asparagus

1 1/2 cups balsamic vinegar

1 shallot, chopped

Zest of 1/2 lemon, cut into thin strips

8 whole black peppercorns

4 tablespoons sweet butter

Salt and freshly ground black pepper

1/4 pound Parmigiano-Reggiano

1. Using a vegetable peeler, scrape the lower third of the asparagus stalks, removing the green.

2. Asparagus is best when cooked al dente, about 3 minutes in a steamer. Remove and let rest on a warm plate.

3. In a small, acid-resistant saucepan, mix the balsamic vinegar, shallot, lemon zest, and black peppercorns. Over medium heat, bring to a boil and simmer, stirring frequently, until reduced by three-quarters. Strain and set aside.

4. In a large sauté pan over high heat, brown the butter. Be careful that it doesn't smoke or burn. Next, add the asparagus and the balsamic syrup. Stir until the asparagus is glazed, and then season to taste and move to a warmed serving platter. Pour the remaining balsamic syrup from the pan over the asparagus.

5. Using your vegetable peeler, shave the Parmigiano-Reggiano around and on top of the asparagus. Serve immediately.

Chef's Recommendation: Syrah

RALPH

Bistro Ralph
Healdsburg
Ralph Tingle
Chef/Owner

Shaved Raw Artichokes, Fava Beans & Parmesan

SERVES 4

1 pound fresh fava beans

8 baby artichokes

Juice of 1 lemon

$1/2$ cup extra virgin olive oil

$1/2$ teaspoon salt

$1/4$ teaspoon coarsely ground black pepper

1 small piece Parmesan cheese, shaved into thin strips with a vegetable peeler

1. Remove the fava beans from their pods. Bring a large pot of water to a boil. Blanch the beans in boiling water for 1 minute and then immerse in ice water to cool. Peel remaining shell from the beans.

2. Remove and discard the dark-green outer leaves from the artichokes. Slice the artichokes paper thin with a very sharp knife. Place in a bowl with the lemon juice and olive oil. Toss to completely coat with the olive oil.

3. Drain the excess oil from the artichokes and toss the artichokes with the fava beans. Season with the salt and pepper. Place on serving plate and top with the shaved Parmesan.

Chef's Recommendation: Colle dei Bardellini, Pigato 1997

Rose Pistola

Rose Pistola
San Francisco
Reed Hearon
Chef/Owner

Southwestern Asparagus, Corn & Tomatillo Soup

SERVES 6

1 tablespoon canola or light olive oil

2 yellow onions, peeled and sliced into thin crescents

2 cloves garlic, minced

¼ cup sherry

1 tablespoon ground cumin

2 bay leaves

1 bunch asparagus, tough stems removed, sliced to 1-inch lengths

2 ears corn, kernels cut from the cob

4 to 6 tomatillos, with the papery cover removed

2 quarts vegetable stock

4 tablespoons yellow or white miso

¼ teaspoon cayenne, plus more to taste

½ cup cilantro leaves, roughly chopped

½ cup flat-leaf parsley leaves, roughly chopped

1 tablespoon fresh oregano or marjoram

Salt to taste

Cashew Cream (see sidebar)

1. Heat the oil in a large, heavy pot and sauté the onions and garlic over medium heat until softened and light brown, about 5 to 7 minutes. Add the sherry followed by the cumin and bay leaves.

2. Add the asparagus, corn, tomatillos, and vegetable stock. Cover and simmer for 20 minutes. The asparagus and tomatillos should be very soft.

3. Remove the bay leaves. Add the miso and cayenne, and puree the soup in batches, adding some of the cilantro, parsley, and oregano to each batch. Return the soup to the soup pot or to a serving bowl and adjust the salt.

4. Serve each portion with 1 tablespoon Cashew Cream.

Chef's Recommendation: good light beer such as wheat or Pilsner

A great spring soup with a unique and complex combination of flavors. The asparagus and tomatillo flavors are highlighted, as are the fresh cilantro and oregano, which are blended into the soup at the end to give the soup brighter color and deeper flavor. We round out the soup with a dollop of cashew cream.

Cashew Cream

½ cup raw cashews

⅔ cup water

1 tablespoon yellow or white miso

1 teaspoon ground nutmeg

Combine all ingredients in a blender and blend until smooth.

Millennium
San Francisco
Eric Tucker
Head Chef

Tomato Concasse

makes about ¹/₂ cup

1 medium-size firm, ripe tomato

Prepare a medium-size bowl of ice water and set aside. Bring a medium-size pot of water to a boil and add a pinch of salt. Core the tomato by making a cone-shaped cut from the stem end with a sharp paring knife. Then cut a small X on the bottom.

(continued next page)

Lark Creek Inn
Larkspur
Bradley Ogden
Chef/Co-owner

Spring Vegetable Soup

SERVES 4

2 tablespoons olive oil

¹/₃ cup diced carrot

²/₃ cup diced yellow Spanish onion

¹/₃ cup fresh corn, cut from the cob

¹/₃ cup diced red potato, skin on

1 teaspoon minced garlic

3 cups Chicken or Turkey Stock (see next page) or tomato juice

Kosher salt to taste

¹/₂ cup Tomato Concasse (see sidebar)

¹/₃ cup diced zucchini

¹/₃ cup sugar snap peas or snow peas, strings removed and cut into ¹/₄-inch pieces

¹/₂ teaspoon chopped fresh tarragon

¹/₂ teaspoon chopped fresh basil

Parmesan cheese or Parmesan Croutons (see next page)

1. Heat the olive oil in a medium-size saucepan over moderate heat. Add the diced carrot, onion, corn, and potato and cook covered for 5 minutes, stirring frequently. Stir in the minced garlic and cook for 1 minute.

2. Add the Chicken or Turkey Stock and salt, and bring to a boil. Lower the heat and add the Tomato Concasse, zucchini, and peas. Simmer gently for 5 minutes or until the vegetables are just tender. Sprinkle on the chopped herbs and simmer for 1 minute longer.

3. Serve immediately in hot soup bowls with shavings of Parmesan cheese or Parmesan Croutons.

Chef's Recommendation: Sauvignon Blanc, Voss, Napa

Chicken or Turkey Stock

makes about 1 gallon

5¹/₂ pounds of chicken or turkey parts in any combination of wings, legs, necks, and carcasses, cut into 3-inch pieces; be sure to include some meat

1 leek, white part only, washed carefully and cut into 1-inch pieces

2 medium yellow Spanish onions, cut into quarters

4 medium carrots, peeled and roughly chopped

4 celery stalks, washed and roughly chopped

2 bay leaves

16 parsley stems, not leaves

1 tablespoon fresh cracked black pepper

1. *Combine all ingredients in a large stockpot with 5 quarts cold water. Bring to a boil. Reduce heat, skim foam from the surface, and simmer, uncovered, for 2 hours. Skim fat and foam from the surface occasionally to ensure a clear stock.*

2. *Strain the stock through a fine strainer. Skim off fat by using a degreasing cup or chilling the stock and removing the solidified fat from the top. Refrigerate or freeze.*

Parmesan Croutons

makes 2 cups

6 small cloves garlic, peeled and crushed

¹/₄ cup unsalted butter

2 cups French bread, cut into ³/₄-inch cubes

¹/₂ cup grated Parmesan cheese

1. *Preheat oven to 350°F.*

2. *Combine the garlic and butter in a small saucepan and cook over moderate heat until the butter has completely melted and is bubbling but not browning. Remove from the heat and let stand for 15 minutes. Strain the butter and discard the garlic cloves.*

3. *Toss the bread and butter together in a bowl, evenly coating the cubes. Place the bread cubes on a sheet pan and bake for 15 minutes. Stir them 2 or 3 times while baking. Once the croutons have become a deep golden brown and are crisp all the way through, remove them from the oven and place them in a large bowl.*

4. *Toss the Parmesan cheese with the croutons while they are still warm.*

(Tomato Concasse continued)

Drop the tomato into boiling salted water for 10 seconds. Immediately remove the tomato and immerse in the ice water to stop the cooking.

Peel the tomato and cut it in half. Over a bowl, carefully squeeze each tomato half to remove the seeds and juice, leaving the tomato intact as much as possible. If you like, reserve the seeds and juice for stocks or soups. Cut the tomato into ¹/₄-inch cubes.

Provençal Vegetable Ragout

SERVES 4

¹/₂ pound pancetta, cut in 1-inch cubes

1 small leek, cut in rings

1 bunch thyme, tied together tightly with string

1 cup chicken stock

1 quart water

8 to 10 baby carrots, peeled, tops left on (if available)

¹/₂ cup spring onions or pearl onions

¹/₂ cup chanterelles or other forest mushrooms

2 cups freshly hulled English peas

12 spears medium asparagus

2 tablespoons unsalted butter

1. Heat a small saucepan over medium heat. Add the pancetta, and brown slowly on all sides, about 5 minutes. Add the leek and the thyme, and cook until the leek begins to soften. Add the chicken stock and water, bring to a boil, reduce to low heat, and simmer, uncovered, for 1 hour or until the pancetta is tender.

2. Remove the thyme and transfer the mixture to a saucepan that is large enough to hold all the vegetables. At this point, there should be about 1 cup of liquid remaining.

3. Bring the heat up to medium and add the carrots, onions, and mushrooms to the pancetta-leek mixture. Cover and cook for about 4 minutes. Add the peas, cover again, and cook for 2 minutes. Add the asparagus and butter and cook for 4 more minutes or until the asparagus and carrots are tender. Be careful not to let the liquid evaporate completely — you may need to add a bit of water along the way. When the ragout is finished, there should be only a small amount of liquid coating the vegetables.

Chef's Recommendation: Sangiovese

Restaurant LuLu
San Francisco
Jody Denton
Chef/Partner

Asparagus & Buttermilk Soup

SERVES 6

1 medium onion, sliced fine

2 peeled shallots, sliced fine

2 cloves garlic, crushed

1 medium potato, sliced fine

6 tablespoons sweet butter

1¼ pounds asparagus, trimmed of white roots and sliced thick (reserve
  some of the tips to be blanched and used for garnish)

Salt and pepper

Buttermilk, about ¼ cup

Chives, chopped

1. In a nonreactive pot, place onions, shallots, garlic, potato, butter, and
   enough water to just cover the vegetables. Bring to a simmer and stir
   occasionally until potatoes are soft. If water evaporates during simmering, add a bit more to cover.

2. Add asparagus to the pot and enough water to just cover the vegetables.
   Bring to a boil, stirring so nothing sticks. When asparagus is soft but
   still slightly crunchy, puree as quickly as possible with a food mill,
   processor, or blender. Moving quickly will ensure a bright-green color
   and fresh asparagus flavor.

3. Pour pureed soup into a stainless steel bowl and place that bowl into a
   larger bowl filled with ice. Chill thoroughly. Season with salt and pepper
   to taste. Gradually add buttermilk to taste, using enough to give the
   soup a dose of acidity but not enough to overpower the asparagus flavor.
   Serve chilled, with chives and blanched asparagus tips.

Chef's Recommendation: Sauvignon Blanc, Sevesiu, Marlborough, NZ

**Restaurant
Sent Sovi**
Saratoga
David Kinch
Chef/Owner

This recipe is very regional and seasonal. The oysters must be fresh, so buy from a reliable source.

Glazed Oysters with Leek Fondue

SERVES 6 AS A FIRST COURSE

30 oysters in the shell; buy Hog Island, Kumamoto, or whatever is best at the market

1 large leek, white and light-green parts only, split lengthwise, washed thoroughly under cool running water, and sliced ⅛-inch thick

½ cup plus 2 tablespoons clam juice

½ cup dry white wine: Chardonnay, Fumé Blanc, or champagne

½ cup Fish Fumet (see next page)

2 shallots, minced

Sprig of thyme

1 bay leaf

4 tablespoons heavy cream

4 tablespoons unsalted butter

Rock salt or kosher salt

1. To open oysters, place a clean towel on a cutting board, arranging the towel to allow an oyster to sit level with the flat shell facing upward. Pry the shells apart by forcing your oyster knife or can opener into the narrowest part of the shell. Catch all juices that drain from the oyster. Once pried open, you must lay your knife flat and sever the abductor muscle. This is done by running the knife flush with the shell. With the top lid free, tip the oyster so it is hanging out. Do this over a bowl and strainer. With the tip of your knife, tease the oyster over the abductor muscle. Scrape abductor muscle into the sauce. Decant and strain the juices. Reserve bottom shells.

2. In a sauté pan, combine the leek and 2 tablespoons of the clam juice (or use water and a pinch of salt). Gently cook until tender and all juices have concentrated, about 15 minutes. This may be done ahead.

3. Preheat oven to 350°F.

GARY DANKO

Gary Danko
San Francisco
Gary Danko
Chef/Owner

4. To make the sauce, combine the liquid gathered from the oysters, wine, $1/2$ cup of the clam juice, fumet, shallots, thyme, and bay leaf in a saucepan. Bring to a boil, reduce heat, and simmer until reduced by one-third. Add cream and return to a boil. Whisk in butter. Strain. Add the leek and bring back to just under a boil.

5. To serve, place the oyster shells on a sheet pan filled with rock salt. Make sure the shells are level. Place in oven for approximately 10 minutes. Heat the sauce gently. Add the oysters and bring to a simmer for 30 seconds. Oysters will plump slightly. Spoon oysters into hot shells. You may run them under the broiler to glaze. Arrange on plates filled with clean rock salt. Serve hot.

Chef's Recommendation: Champagne Delamotte, Blanc de Blancs, NV France

Fish Fumet

makes about 3 cups

1 pound bones and trimmings of any white fish such as sole or flounder

1 medium onion, peeled and sliced thin

2 tablespoons fresh lemon juice

$1/2$ teaspoon salt

$1/2$ tablespoon white peppercorns

$1/2$ cup dry white wine

1 bay leaf

In a heavy saucepan, combine the fish bones (be sure the bones are very clean and free of any blood) and trimmings along with the sliced onion, lemon juice, salt, peppercorns, white wine, and bay leaf. Cover the pan and steam the bones over medium-high heat for 5 to 10 minutes.

Add $3 1/2$ cups cold water and bring the liquid to a boil. Skim the froth and simmer the fumet very slowly for 45 minutes. Strain the stock through cheesecloth or a fine-mesh sieve. If you are not using it immediately, cool it thoroughly, cover with plastic wrap, and refrigerate.

Feuilletée of Morels, Artichokes, Roasted Fennel & Fava Beans
with an Asparagus Beurre Blanc

SERVES 6

For the filling:

2 bulbs of fennel, sliced

2 tablespoons olive oil

2 teaspoons minced garlic

$^1/_2$ teaspoon salt

$^1/_4$ teaspoon pepper

1 pound morel mushrooms, cut in half and washed

2 cups peeled and trimmed baby artichokes, cooked

2 cups shucked fava beans, peeled and blanched

1 tablespoon chopped tarragon

For the pastry:

6 five-by-three-inch rectangular pieces of puff pastry

1 egg, beaten

For the beurre blanc:

1 pound asparagus

2 cups cream

$^1/_2$ cup white wine

$^1/_2$ pound butter

Salt and white pepper to taste

1. Preheat oven to 375°F.

2. To make the filling, place the fennel, 1 tablespoon of the olive oil, and 1 teaspoon of the garlic in an ovenproof dish. Mix well, season with salt and pepper, and roast for 10 to 15 minutes until soft. Repeat the same process with the morel mushrooms, using the remaining olive oil and garlic. Cook until the mushrooms are soft. Mix the fennel, mushrooms, artichokes, and fava beans together. Add the tarragon and check the seasoning for salt and pepper.

Lalime's
Berkeley
Frances Wilson
Executive Chef

3. To bake the puffs, place the puff pastry pieces on a baking dish and brush with the beaten egg. Bake until golden brown and puffed up, 25 to 30 minutes.

4. To make the beurre blanc, cut the tips off the asparagus and trim any white from the stems. Blanch the asparagus tips in boiling water for 2 minutes. Remove and set to one side for garnish. Place the asparagus stems in the water and boil until soft. Puree the stems in a food processor until smooth. Rub through a sieve to remove any fibrous parts. Place the cream in a pot, bring to a boil, and simmer gently until the cream has been reduced by half. Place the wine in a separate, nonreactive pot and reduce by half. Combine with the cream. Whisk in the cold butter and then add the asparagus puree. Season with salt and white pepper. Keep hot but don't boil.

5. To assemble, heat the filling in a pot until hot. Split the puff pastry rectangles in half and place the bottom half on a plate. Top with the filling and then cover with the other half of the pastry. Pour some of the sauce around the plate, and garnish with some of the asparagus tips.

Note: If you wish to do a lighter version of this dish, thin the asparagus puree with some vegetable stock instead of using beurre blanc.

Chef's Recommendation: Merlot, Truchard, Napa 1996

Strawberry Soup with Lemon Balm Granita

SERVES 8

For the granita:

1 cup sugar

4 cups water

$^1/_4$ cup fresh lemon juice (Meyer lemon preferred)

1 bunch fresh lemon balm or lemon verbena

For the soup:

2 pint-baskets of strawberries; reserve 4 strawberries for garnish

$^1/_2$ cup fresh orange juice

$^1/_4$ cup fresh lemon juice (Meyer preferred)

$^1/_4$ cup honey

1 cup champagne or seltzer

1. To make the granita, combine the sugar, water, lemon juice, and lemon balm in a nonreactive pan and bring to a boil. Remove from heat and place in the refrigerator until cold. Strain through cheesecloth, wringing it well. Pour the granita into a shallow 8x8-inch pan. Place in the freezer for at least 4 hours, stirring with a fork every 30 minutes to make texture crumbly, or freeze in an ice cream maker according to the manufacturer's directions.

2. To make the strawberry soup, rinse the strawberries, keeping the hulls on, blot well, and reserve 4 of the largest. Puree the balance (with the hulls) in a food processor. Strain puree through an extra-fine mesh strainer. Remove the seeds, and place in a nonreactive pan with the citrus juices and honey. Stir well, bring to a boil, and then, over ice, cool to room temperature or colder. Strain into reserved puree and now discard seeds and hulls. Chill in the refrigerator until serving time.

3. Just before serving, coarsely chop the reserved strawberries. Stir the champagne or seltzer into the strawberry base. Ladle into chilled, clear glass bowls; top with about 2 heaping tablespoons of granita; and garnish with the chopped strawberries.

Chef's Recommendation: White Riesling, Navarro Cluster Select, Anderson Valley 1997

Lalime's
Berkeley
Judith Maguire
Pastry Chef

Asparagus Salad
with Meyer Lemon Vinaigrette

SERVES 8

32 jumbo asparagus spears

2 tablespoons olive oil

Salt and freshly ground white pepper to taste

1 pound mesclun greens

Meyer Lemon Vinaigrette (see sidebar)

4 ounces Parmigiano-Reggiano

1. Preheat oven to 450°F.

2. Rinse the asparagus, and then break off the woody ends by holding the spear near its base and, starting about an inch or 2 higher, bending it with your other hand until the spear snaps; if it doesn't break, just keep moving gradually up the stalk, bending as you go, until it does. Lightly pare the tips with a vegetable peeler to remove any remaining tough skin. Discard the woody ends.

3. Toss the asparagus with the olive oil and divide between 2 cookie sheets, a single layer in each. Sprinkle generously with the salt and white pepper. Bake 10 minutes until the spears are done al dente. Transfer to a chilled cookie sheet, cover loosely with wax paper, and refrigerate until cold.

4. On the bias, cut jumbo asparagus spears into thin oblong disks. Toss greens and asparagus with 1 cup of the vinaigrette. Divide among 8 chilled plates.

5. Top with the cheese, shaved into long, thin strips with a vegetable peeler. Serve immediately.

Chef's Recommendation: Sauvignon Blanc, Spottswoode

Meyer Lemon Vinaigrette

1 teaspoon lemon zest, finely chopped

1/2 cup freshly squeezed lemon juice, preferably from Meyer lemons

1 tablespoon Dijon mustard

1 dash Tabasco

1/2 cup extra virgin olive oil

1/2 cup canola oil

Salt and freshly ground black pepper to taste

To make the vinaigrette, in a nonreactive bowl whisk together the lemon zest, lemon juice, mustard, Tabasco, and oils. Season with salt and pepper to taste. Set aside.

Bittersweet Bistro
Aptos
Thomas Vinolus
Chef/Proprietor

Chocolate-Dipped Strawberries

Approximately 8 ounces dipping chocolate (don't use molding or tempered chocolate)

1 pint organic strawberries, with stems intact

Chop the chocolate into small cubes and place in a small stainless steel bowl that fits snugly within a small pot. Fill the pot with enough water to touch the bottom of the bowl and create a hot-water bath. Make sure the bowl doesn't float and that water can't splash into the chocolate. Place over low

(continued next page)

Mixx
Santa Rosa
Kathleen Berman
Pastry Chef/
Proprietor

Almond Tart with Fresh Berries
& Fresh Strawberry Ice Cream

SERVES 10 (ONE 9-INCH TART)

For tart dough: (makes enough for three 9-inch tarts)

6 ounces granulated sugar (about $^3/_4$ cup)

14 ounces unsalted butter, room temperature

1 egg

$^1/_2$ teaspoon vanilla extract

1 pound all-purpose flour (about $3^1/_3$ cups)

For the almond filling:

4 ounces almond paste at room temperature

4 ounces sweet butter at room temperature

$^1/_2$ cup sugar

2 large eggs at room temperature

To finish:

Fresh berries, such as strawberries (halved or quartered depending on size), raspberries, or blackberries for garnish

Apricot Glaze (available at Mixx Pastry and Accessories and at gourmet food stores)

Fresh Strawberry Ice Cream (see next page)

Chocolate-Dipped Strawberries (see sidebar)

The day before serving:

1. Using the hook attachment, combine the sugar, butter, egg, and vanilla in a Kitchen Aid mixer. When well blended, add the flour all at once. Mix until just combined; don't overmix. Remove the dough from the bowl and separate into thirds. Wrap and freeze 2 portions for later use. Take the remaining portion and lightly press and shape it into a disk with the heel of your hand. Wrap the dough in plastic wrap, and refrigerate overnight.

On the day of serving:

2. Preheat oven to 375°F.

3. On a lightly floured board, gently roll out dough so that it is $^1/_4$-inch thick and 2 inches larger than tart pan; use a flat dish or platter as a

guide. Carefully fold the dough in half and gently place it in a 9-inch tart pan with a removable bottom (the dough should stand about $^1/_2$ inch above the tart-pan rim). Prick bottom of dough with a fork, and chill in the refrigerator. When ready to bake, line the bottom with aluminum foil and spread with a layer of raw dried beans or rice. Bake until half done, about 10 minutes.

4. As tart dough first chills and then bakes, prepare almond filling. In a small bowl, mix almond paste and butter at medium speed. Almond paste and butter must be the same temperature to create a smooth filling. Add sugar and then add eggs, one at a time, beating after each, but only until just combined. Do not overbeat.

5. Reduce oven heat to 350°F.

6. Fill partially baked tart shell with almond mixture. Bake until top of tart is light golden brown, about 20 minutes. Cool. Garnish with fresh whole or halved berries, and brush rim of tart with apricot glaze. (Do not glaze raspberries and blackberries.) Serve with Fresh Strawberry Ice Cream and Chocolate-Dipped Strawberries.

Chef's Recommendation: White Riesling, Navarro Cluster Select, Anderson Valley 1997

Fresh Strawberry Ice Cream

serves 4 to 6

$^1/_2$ pound fresh organic strawberries, after stems are removed

$^3/_4$ cup granulated sugar

1 cup heavy whipping cream

Chocolate-Dipped Strawberries, for garnish (see sidebar)

1. *Place strawberries and sugar in food processor with chopping blade in place. Pulse mixture and scrape down the sides of the bowl. Run the food processor until the sugar is dissolved and the mixture is no longer gritty.*

2. *Pour in cream. Run processor until the mixture thickens slightly and bubbles pop slowly on top. Do not overprocess. The result should be creamy, not chalky. Use the pulse switch as the mixture nears the proper texture.*

3. *Turn mixture into an ice cream machine. Process according to manufacturer's instructions; place in freezer until firm.*

4. *Serve in martini glasses on dessert plates with doilies or on the Almond Tart with Fresh Berries. Garnish with fresh whole strawberries or with Chocolate-Dipped Strawberries for extra flair.*

(Chocolate-Dipped Strawberries continued)

heat and stir gently as the chocolate begins to melt. When chocolate is almost fully melted, remove from heat and continue stirring until smooth and satiny.

Making sure they are completely dry and cool, dip the strawberries in the warm chocolate. Place them on a parchment-lined cookie sheet or flat platter and refrigerate until the chocolate sets. Store at room temperature. Chocolate-dipped strawberries should be eaten within 24 hours.

Spring Lamb Chops
with Fava-Mashed Potatoes

FOR EACH PERSON:

Small rack or loin lamb chops, about $1/2$-inch thick and trimmed of all but $1/8$ inch of fat

Sea salt

$1/2$ pound fava beans

3 tablespoons onion, finely diced

2 sage leaves

2 tablespoons olive oil

$1/4$ to $1/3$ pound new red creamer or fingerling potatoes

1. Several hours before cooking, season lamb liberally overall with sea salt and refrigerate.

2. Shell the favas by removing the fat, fleshy seeds from their padded casing. Next, peel away the outer skin, which resembles nothing more than a bit of rubber glove! This is a little tedious, but if you carve away the tip of the seed with a tiny knife or your fingernail, you can usually remove the rest of the skin in a few seconds. Resist the temptation to blanch the favas and then pop them out of their skins—they won't cook down into the earthy mash I am looking for.

3. Set the raw favas to stew in a deep, heavy pot with the onions, sage leaves (which you should bruise just before adding to the pot), olive oil, and sea salt to taste. The vegetables should be at least 3 inches deep. Cover tightly and cook on the lowest possible flame until the favas start to decompose. Don't add water—the onion should contribute enough moisture. Stir every 10 minutes or so.

4. Wash the new potatoes, trim any green spots or wounds, and then cut into bite-size nuggets. Cook until tender in vigorously boiling, well-salted water. Drain and mash, skins and all, with a potato masher.

5. Gently combine the mashed potatoes with the softened favas. Taste. Add sea salt and more warmed olive oil to taste. Keep warm while you cook the skinny lamb chops over very hot coals or in a searing-hot cast-iron pan with a film of olive oil.

Chef's Recommendation: Pinot Noir or Chianti

Zuni
San Francisco
Judy Rodgers
Chef/Owner

Just-Baked Wild Boysenberry Shortcake

SERVES 6

2 cups self-rising flour

1 teaspoon salt

$^1/_3$ cup sugar, plus additional for dipping shortcakes

1 to 1$^1/_2$ cups heavy cream

$^1/_2$ cup melted butter

3 pints fresh wild boysenberries, cleaned (use strawberries if you can't find boysenberries)

1 tablespoon fresh lemon juice

Simple Syrup (see sidebar)

Vanilla ice cream or whipped cream, for serving

1. Preheat oven to 425°F.

2. Combine the flour, salt, and sugar in a mixing bowl. Stir those dry ingredients with a fork to blend. Slowly add 1 cup of the cream to the mixture, stirring constantly.

3. Gather the dough together. If dough seems dry and won't hold together, add more cream. When it holds together but isn't sticky, turn out onto an ungreased baking sheet and pat into a 1-inch-high square.

4. Cut the large square into 6 biscuits. Dip biscuits in melted butter and then in sugar, coating thoroughly.

5. Bake 15 to 20 minutes until golden brown.

6. Crush one-third of the berries and mix with the lemon juice and 2 to 3 tablespoons of Simple Syrup. In a separate bowl, toss the remaining berries with 2 to 3 more tablespoons of Simple Syrup.

7. Slice the warm shortcakes in half. Sandwich the crushed berries between biscuits, and top with the whole berries and whipped cream or ice cream.

Chef's Recommendation: Bonny Doon vin de Glacière 1997

Simple Syrup

$^1/_2$ cup sugar

$^1/_4$ cup water

1 teaspoon vanilla

Combine the sugar, water, and vanilla in a small saucepan. Bring to a boil, stirring often. When the syrup reaches a boil, remove the pan from the heat. Set aside and cool.

Boulevard
San Francisco
Nancy Oakes
Chef/Owner

Ragout of Spring Vegetables
with Aged Sherry Vinegar & Green Olive Oil

SERVES 6

Green olive oil is also called fall harvest. Good California producers include Sciabica and Da Vero (harder to find).

Buy whatever vegetables are best, and don't worry if you cannot find them all.

1 bunch baby carrots, peeled

1 bunch baby gold beets

1 bunch baby chiogga beets

1 bunch baby turnips

1 bunch baby leeks, trimmed, whites only

1 pound baby artichokes, trimmed

6 cups Vegetable Stock (see sidebar on next page)

¾ cup white table wine

¼ cup olive oil

1 medium celery root, peeled

1 large Yukon Gold potato, peeled

2 teaspoons salt

Aged sherry vinegar to taste

Green olive oil to taste

1 bunch chives, snipped into ¼-inch pieces

Chive blossoms (optional)

Freshly ground black pepper

1. In separate pots of salted boiling water, cook the carrots, beets, turnips, and leeks until still slightly crisp. Remove and cool on a sheet pan lined with parchment paper. Peel the turnips and beets and cut in half.

2. Cook the artichokes in 3 cups of the Vegetable Stock, the white wine, and the olive oil until tender. Set aside to cool. Remove artichokes from cooking stock. Stock can be discarded or saved.

3. With a small melon baller, cut out celery root and potato rounds. Cook in heavily salted boiling water (2 tablespoons of salt to 2 quarts of water) until still slightly crisp. Drain and cool.

restaurant
ELISABETH DANIEL

Elisabeth Daniel
San Francisco
Daniel Patterson
Chef/Owner

4. In a nonreactive pot, heat the blanched carrots, turnips, leeks, and beets in the remaining Vegetable Stock. Add salt, bring to a simmer, and cook for 1 minute. Add the artichokes, celery root, and potatoes. Cook for 1 minute more, until they are thoroughly heated.

5. Remove vegetables with a slotted spoon and divide evenly among 6 soup plates. Put plates in a 300°F oven to keep warm, and season the remaining Vegetable Stock with sherry vinegar, green olive oil, and salt, if necessary. Remove plates from the oven and put an equal amount of seasoned stock over each. Garnish with chives, chive blossoms, and freshly ground black pepper.

Chef's Recommendation: Pouilly Fumé, Domaine Dageneau les Berthiers 1995

Vegetable Stock

1 1/2 medium yellow onions, sliced

1/2 onion, charred over an open flame

2 carrots, peeled and sliced

1/2 head of fennel, sliced

1 leek, sliced

1/3 head of celery root, peeled and sliced

1/3 bunch thyme

Put all ingredients in a nonreactive stockpot. Cover with water (be sure to add at least 7 cups of water). Bring to a boil and simmer for 1 hour. Strain through a fine-mesh sieve.

**Local Foods
Local Flavors**

DaVero Olive Oil *produces oil from four types of olive trees native to Tuscany. Co-owners Colleen McGlynn and Ridgely Evers imported and began planting cuttings from these varietals in 1990 and now have more than 4,500 trees on more than 20 acres. In Italian,* davvero *is used colloquially to mean* this is the best, the real thing.

*e*XPLORING THE PROBLEMS OF
MODERN FOOD PRODUCTION

BAY AREA SUMMER CROPS

APRICOTS

ARUGULA

ASIAN PEARS

BASIL

BEETS

BLACKBERRIES

BLUEBERRIES

BOYSENBERRIES

BROCCOLI

BUTTER BEANS

CARROTS

CAULIFLOWER

CIPPOLINI ONIONS

CRANBERRY BEANS

CROOKNECK SQUASH

CUCUMBER

EGGPLANT

FENNEL

FIGS

FRISEE

GARLIC

GRAPES

HASS AVOCADOS

HERBS

LEEKS

LETTUCE

LIMA BEANS

MACHE

MELONS

MIZUNA

MULBERRIES

MUSTARD GREENS

NECTARINES

OKRA

ONIONS

PATTYPAN SQUASH

PEACHES

PEPPERS

PLUMS

POTATOES

RADICCHIO

RASPBERRIES

SHELL BEANS

SNAP BEANS

STRAWBERRIES

SWEET CORN

TOMATOES

TREVISO

TURNIPS

ZUCCHINI

As much as I love the fresh aromas and tenderness of new spring crops, there is something special about summer. It's an artistic time: A time of exotic color and mouthwatering flavors. A time to imagine the smooth skin of a truly vine-ripe tomato or the firm purple skin of a baby Japanese eggplant. A time when hordes of customers crowd the farmers market hoping to pick melons as good as the one they just tasted at our table. A time when sweet, ribbed, crunchy Armenian and Japanese cucumbers form the basis of the mouthwatering Greek salads of high summer, and the little baby squash lend the first summer color in the kitchen.

It's a time when the mind has almost no resistance; it just flows with the colors, flavors, and textures of the thousands of varieties the farm has to offer. Who needs genetically engineered foods when the forces of nature are so naturally prolific? When there are farmers market extravaganzas, where shoppers go crazy over the mountains of heirloom tomatoes—at least 25 to 30 varieties on any given summer day? When Thai, Persian lemon, and Genovese basil are on hand? And when fantastic menus grace fantastic restaurants?

As long as farmers watch their water, fertilizer, and plant-stress levels, it's hard not to produce great-tasting crops. In farming, you can go for flavor or you can go for volume. You're not always going to get volume when you shoot for flavor. When you hold off on water to intensify the flavor of melons, tomatoes, or cucumbers, they can suffer from sunscald. Certain varieties of peppers don't have the amount of foliage cover some of the new hybrids do. There are techniques that can overcome those drawbacks, such as covering melons with straw or growing beans with peppers. They can be difficult to do on large farms, but can be done on smaller farms or in home gardens. That's why knowing your farmers and how they farm is important if you care about flavor and freshness.

I don't see the need for the work being done on plant breeding when there is so much diversity already. A lot of the new breeds equal nothing more than pounds per acre, which translates into cheap food for a fast-food- and cosmetic-obsessed food world. One more perfect-looking bell pepper is not going to solve food shortages worldwide.

The truth about our fast-food world is becoming more and more evident as the organic industry grows. So buy local, buy fresh, and buy flavor. Follow the basics of sustainability. Eat seasonally. With the wealth of incredible produce available here in California, you can be transported anywhere on the Mediterranean or to Provence with just one visit to your local farmers market, wine merchant, and bakery. With your sweetheart close by, and the beautiful Pacific and central coast on hand, how can you go wrong?

A Taste of Summer

STONE FREE FARM

Stone Free Farm specializes in organic root, leaf, and specialty vegetables as well as melons and tomatoes. It farms 360 acres that are spilt among three climate zones, and it operates the only all-organic roadside stand in the tricounty area. Stone Free Farm believes that organic food is essential to our physical and mental health, our environment, and the well-being of our children.

by **Stuart Dickson**
Stone Free Farm
Watsonville,
California

By almost every measure, the past 40 years have been a triumph of agricultural technology. Productivity on America's farms has increased eight times over. From 1930 to 1980, the amount of tomatoes grown per acre climbed from 4 to 24 tons. The yield of an acre of corn jumped from 21 to 91 bushels. The average American farmer now produces annually enough food for 128 people, supplying 40 percent of the world's corn and half of the world's soybeans.

The Growing Danger of Monocropping

Yet the apparent triumph of the so-called green revolution has come at a steep price. Indeed, many experts now say that modern agricultural methods contain the seeds of a catastrophe that could devastate the world's agriculture and even lead to famine.

Depleting the Soil, Draining the Water

The danger begins with the soil itself. Modern agricultural methods depend on the widespread use of chemical fertilizers, which have helped drive the astonishing productivity of today's corporate farms. By using chemical fertilizers, farmers no longer need to leave fields fallow or rotate crops to replenish soil. The same areas can be planted year after year after year. And once a crop is harvested, fields are tilled under, the weeds eradicated by using herbicides, and the soil left bare through the winter until the next crop is planted.

For all its efficiency, however, the method leaves topsoil bare and unprotected from the wind during the fallow months. As a result, in many parts of the world there has been a steady erosion of topsoil. Iowa, for instance, with some of the most fertile soil in the world, has lost half of its topsoil; roughly 4 inches has simply blown and washed away since 1900. Two and a half million acres of cropland in the United States are abandoned each year because of soil degradation. Worldwide, 30 percent of total arable land has been lost due to erosion in the past 40 years.

And when soil erodes, water can't be absorbed into the ground as easily, which causes run-off and increases the amount of water farmers need for irrigation. In some parts of Kansas, Oklahoma, and Texas, farmers are pumping water out of underground aquifers faster than it can be replenished. Eventually, the well may simply run dry. "These are losses that could take centuries to undo," says David Pimentel, professor of ecology and agricultural sciences at Cornell University.

Water and soil aren't the only worries. Most of today's chemical fertilizers and pesticides are made of petroleum, a limited resource. The equivalent of 140 gallons of oil is necessary to manufacture the chemicals used for growing an acre of corn. Eventually, experts like Pimentel say,

by Peter Jaret

supplies will run out—or become so expensive that they drastically raise the price of food around the world.

Stewart Smith, who studies agricultural economics at the University of Maine, puts the case bluntly: "Current farming methods—as productive as they have been—simply can't be sustained."

Monoculture Shock

Unfortunately, there's even more trouble down on the nation's farm. A century ago, most American farms were small, family-run operations. A typical farmer grew a variety of crops on a relatively small amount of acreage—from corn and tomatoes to melons and beans. At the end of each growing season, seeds were saved to be planted again in the spring. Over time, farmers developed their own unique varieties, called landraces, which were particularly well suited to the conditions of a certain region, even a single farm—from temperature and annual rainfall to number of daylight hours and length of the growing season.

No longer. For one thing, large farming operations have abandoned genetically diverse landraces for a small handful of hybrid varieties. As these commercially produced seeds have dominated the market, crops like corn, wheat, and potatoes have begun to look as genetically alike as identical twins. Moreover, as corporate farms have swallowed up the traditional small farmer, vast tracts of these genetically similar crops, called monocultures, have been planted. Now, thousands of acres may be planted in exactly the same kind of wheat or corn or soybeans.

That could spell disaster. "The engineered crops of today are fickle thoroughbreds, honed for short-term performance and profit, not long-term health," say Martin Teitel and Hope Shand, authors of *The Ownership of Life*. "The resulting loss of genetic diversity leaves the entire seed supply vulnerable to climate change, pests, and disease."

In the past, the wide variety of genetic strains represented by landraces and the planting of small fields of similar crops created a natural defense against pests and disease: If a plant virus or a fungus suddenly appeared, it could spread only so far and no farther. One variety of corn might be vulnerable, but another would be immune. As monocropping has taken over, though, that defense has disappeared. Now if that same new pest or plant disease emerges, it's likely to wipe out immense fields of genetically identical plants. As Garrison Wilkes, professor of ecology at the University of Massachusetts in Boston, says, "The danger with such large monoculture crops is that when a disease or pest comes along, huge amounts of acres can go down when a crash occurs."

Dress rehearsals of disaster have already occurred. In 1970 a disease

Regional Family Farms

Select Sonoma County certifies SONOMA GROWN™ and SONOMA MADE™ products. It humbly bills itself as a nonprofit agricultural marketing organization for Sonoma County's agricultural producers, but lovers of fine food know that when they see the SONOMA GROWN™ or SONOMA MADE™ label, they're getting the highest-quality agricultural products from one of the country's greatest food and wine regions.

called southern corn leaf blight struck Florida's corn crop, wiping out the equivalent of 1 billion bushels—15 percent of the biggest U.S. crop. The blight spread as far and as fast as it did, say experts, because virtually all commercial corn varieties are so genetically alike and because vast tracts of monocultures enabled the blight to spread far and wide.

In 1990 a fungus called phytophtora began to infect New England's potato crops—the same disease that created devastating famines in Ireland a century and a half ago. By 1994 the potato blight had destroyed nearly one-quarter of Maine's potato crop. Since then, it has spread through the East and Midwest, and not long after that the blight hit Idaho and Oregon, where most U.S. potato production is centered. "So far, we've been able to control it in many areas by using more fungicides," says Kenneth Deahl, a researcher at the U.S. Department of Agriculture. "But each year the damage increases."

Small wonder. Idaho russet potatoes, which represent 90 percent of the nation's crop, have no resistance at all.

The looming crisis is all the more urgent as the world's population increases. Within the next 10 years, there will be 800 million more mouths to feed. By the year 2100, researchers say, the United States will need to increase agricultural productivity sixfold in order to keep up. A huge crash of monoculture crops could lead to a sweeping catastrophe.

Desperately Seeking Solutions

What can be done to avert disaster? One solution, of course, would be a return to the traditional farming practice of planting a patchwork of different crops rather than monocultures. Another would be the readoption of traditional sustainable farming methods, which do not rely on the use of tons of chemicals.

But getting there won't be easy. "The notion of going back to a simpler, more traditional way of farming may be comforting," says Dennis Avery, director of the Center for Global Food Issues at the Hudson Institute, "but it's a luxury few places in the world can afford." Organic farming, he contends, typically requires about twice the acreage to produce the same amount of food as high-tech methods. The United States uses only 6 million acres to grow the crops we need. A return to organic methods would require using twice that amount, which would mean cutting down huge areas of wilderness.

"The real challenge of the 21st century isn't producing enough food," says Avery. "It's feeding the world without doubling or tripling the amount of land used for crops. One option we don't have is to go backward."

Advocates of organic farming aren't so sure. In truth, no one really knows how productive traditional methods could be because so little research has been done. For the past 50 years, the emphasis has been almost entirely on manufacturing new chemical fertilizers, pesticides, and herbicides. "Given a serious investment in organic farming research," says Smith, "it's very likely we could find ways to use less land to produce more." Indeed, traditional methods will almost have to be part of the solution if we are to achieve a truly sustainable agriculture, some experts say.

Some growers are already taking important steps in that direction. Not long ago, the federal government called for the wider use of integrated pest management (IPM)—an approach that borrows from the traditional methods of farming to substantially decrease reliance on chemical pesticides. The goal is to use IPM on 75 percent of U.S. cropland by 2000. But as many as half of the nation's farms may already use at least some of those methods. For example, more than 90 percent of the apple growers in Washington State use some IPM methods to control pests and diseases, thereby substantially reducing the amount of pesticides and herbicides required.

That represents significant progress. The nation's agriculture system doesn't have to shift wholesale to organic farming, after all, to substantially reduce the use of chemicals. According to Pimentel, even simple changes in farming methods could slash by half the amount of pesticides used—and without affecting yield or quality. The same is true around the world.

Not surprisingly, perhaps, the move toward integrated pest management is being led by the nation's small farmers. Many experts say the small farmer represents the future of sustainable agriculture. For one thing, small farmers don't create monocultures. Instead, they typically grow a variety of crops in a limited area of acreage, thereby providing a natural defense against sweeping epidemics of plant diseases. Small farmers also have the deepest stake in sustainable agriculture. Unlike agribusinesses, which can more easily abandon one set of fields for another, small farmers who deplete the soil are out of business. Small wonder that they are the growers with the keenest interest in finding workable solutions to the profound problems the world faces down on the farm.

Ways to support your local small farmer are to shop at farmers markets and to ask your grocer which produce comes from local growers. An even better way is to join the community-supported-agriculture (CSA) movement. The concept is simple: local consumers invest in a local farmer by paying money up front for fruits and vegetables that are to be harvested during the year. CSA farms offer a chance to see exactly how the produce you eat is grown. Joining the growing CSA movement is also the best way to encourage local farmers who are dedicated to sustainable methods of feeding the world.

Regional Family Farms

SONOMA COUNTY

FARM TRAILS

Sonoma County Farm Trails is a nonprofit trade association dedicated to promoting on-site direct marketing of locally grown or locally processed agricultural products. Formed in 1972, the organization is an active association of farmers who practice direct marketing by opening their farms to the public.

Seeds: Agriculture's Vanishing Heritage

by Hope Shand
Research Director
Rural
Advancement
Foundation
International

The plethora of glossy garden-seed catalogs sent to small farmers and backyard gardeners masks a disturbing trend toward consolidation of the seed industry, a trend that dramatically narrows the availability of nonhybrid vegetable varieties. A wealth of vegetable-seed diversity is being lost forever.

According to the Iowa-based Seed Savers Exchange, nearly half of all nonhybrid vegetable varieties available in 1984 had been dropped from mail-order seed catalogs by 1991. Those losses appear to be accelerating through the 1990s. The Seed Savers Exchange believes the massive shift to hybrid varieties is the leading cause of garden-seed-diversity loss.

Thirty years ago, most North American seed companies were small, family-owned businesses specializing in varieties adapted to regional climates and resistant to local pests and diseases. Today the seeds purchased by farmers are more likely to come from giant, multinational corporations whose names typically are associated with agrochemicals or pharmaceuticals.

Why Worry about Corporate Seeds?

Today the top 10 seed corporations control 30 percent of the $23-billion global seed market. Virtually all of those companies have interests in agrochemicals, and most are engineering plants that are marketed with—or depend on—companion chemicals. Virtually all of the major seed companies produce genetically engineered seeds that can tolerate chemical weed killers. This makes sense for companies that sell both proprietary seeds and herbicides.

Furthermore, giant seed companies operating on a global scale find it more economical to breed genetically uniform varieties that are suited to the needs of commercial agribusiness rather than to the needs of small farmers or backyard gardeners. Corporate breeders are more likely to develop varieties that perform adequately over vast geographic areas rather than for local climates or for resistance to local pests or diseases. And whereas backyard gardeners are looking for better-tasting tomatoes, corporate breeders are more interested in producing varieties with longer shelf life or vegetables that can withstand mechanical harvesting.

Ownership and Control

With the arrival of genetic engineering, seed companies are using monopoly patents to stake far-reaching claims of ownership over crop genes and traits. In the United States, it is now illegal for farmers to save patented seeds and reuse them. One large company has publicly declared it will vigorously prosecute farmers who are caught infringing its patent. In some areas, that company has hired private investigators to root out farmers who are saving its patented seed.

What Can I Do?

Farmers and gardeners who are concerned about control and ownership of seeds can educate themselves and their customers about the implications of seed industry consolidation and the impact on food security. Fortunately, there are many regional seed companies that still offer unique collections of self-pollinated seeds. And you can buy your produce from small farms that are growing varieties suited to your region. If you value diversity, those companies and farmers deserve your support.

Eating with conscience is a powerful tool used to ensure that farm animals be treated as humanely as possible. Most food products obtained from animals raised in the United States come from factorylike farms, where animals are crowded into feedlots and buildings or virtually immobilized in crates and cages. You can demand the humane treatment of farm animals by adopting food-buying strategies that reward farmers who are sensitive to the well-being of animals.

Eating with Conscience

Why eat with conscience? Common sense and compassion offer the most compelling reasons. There are no justifiable reasons to subject farm animals to needless pain and suffering just because they are raised for food. Farmers who practice good animal husbandry methods never follow the common practices of factory farms, such as confining hens so tightly they can't spread their wings or keeping pigs in crates for virtually their entire lives.

Supporting the humane treatment of farm animals is a choice each of us can make with our food dollars. By doing so, we help move society toward a time when animals get treated with consideration and not as disposable commodities. The first step is to find out how the food you purchase is obtained. If you don't know your farmer, check the label. Labels that advertise meat, eggs, or dairy products as free-range, uncaged, or pasture raised indicate that the animals were not tightly confined. The label *certified organic* also indicates animals were treated humanely. If the food you buy does not carry one of those labels, it's more than likely the animals were raised in factory farms.

You can be better assured that you are eating a more humane diet if you shop at natural food stores, food co-ops, and farmers markets and if you subscribe to community-supported-agriculture projects. By buying from local farmers, you have the opportunity to find out how the animals were treated.

by Gary L. Valen
Director of
Sustainable
Agriculture
Humane Society of
the United States

Unblemished Fruits & Vegetables & Pesticide Use

by David Pimentel
Professor of Ecology and Agricultural Sciences
College of Agriculture and Life Sciences
Cornell University
from The Pesticide Question:
Environment, Economics and Ethics

The American marketplace features nearly perfect fruits and vegetables. Gone are the blemished apples, slightly russetted oranges, and fresh spinach with a leaf miner. Also not apparent are the pesticides.

The U.S. Food and Drug Administration, which investigates pesticide residues on foods found in supermarkets, reports that although 97 percent of consumers prefer their food to be pesticide free, about 35 percent of the foods eaten by Americans contain detectable pesticide residues. And 10 to 20 percent of the insecticides and miticides used on fruits and vegetables are there to meet the high cosmetic standards of produce in supermarkets. Moreover, anywhere from 1 to 3 percent of foods that contain pesticide residues are above the legal tolerance level. Unfortunately, therefore, consumers are eating foods with acceptable residue levels and foods that are highly contaminated. And it's not possible to tell which foods are which.

Resources for Living Local

The **Chez Panisse Foundation** was created in 1996 to raise funds for youth and community garden and cooking projects that teach responsible land stewardship and its vital relationship to safe, healthy, and delicious food. The foundation distributes grants and makes contributions to organizations that share the foundation's commitment to promoting sustainable agriculture through education and hands-on participation in gardening and cooking.

CORN SPOON BREAD
  Nancy Oakes, Boulevard 98

LATE SUMMER SALAD: FIGS & MELON WITH GOAT CHEESE & CITRUS VINAIGRETTE
  Annie Somerville, Greens 99

PAN ROAST CHICKEN BREASTS WITH SUMMER SUCCOTASH
  Wendy Brucker, Rivoli 100

MEDITERRANEAN PASTA
  Thomas Vinolus, Bittersweet Bistro 101

ARUGULA SALAD WITH RAW SWEET CORN & SWEET 100 TOMATOES
  Judy Rodgers, Zuni 102

BAKED RED SNAPPER WITH TOMATOES, PEPPERS & ONIONS
  Bradley Ogden, Lark Creek Inn 103

SPICY TUNA, CAPER, ANCHOVY & TOMATO SANDWICHES
  Jesse Cool, Flea Street Café 104

CHOPPED SALAD
  Jody Denton, Restaurant LuLu 105

YELLOW CORN/BRIOCHE PUDDING WITH WHITE TRUFFLE BUTTER
  Daniel Patterson, Elisabeth Daniel 106

SMOKED LAMB & GARLIC SAUSAGE WITH ROASTED RED PEPPER CONFIT
& MUSTARD SAUCE
  Anne Gingrass, Hawthorne Lane 108

GRILLED FISH WITH HEIRLOOM TOMATOES & SALSA VERDE
  Reed Hearon, Rose Pistola 110

GINGER-GLAZED PLUM & WALNUT GALETTE
  Eric Tucker, Millennium 112

ROASTED SALMON WITH OVEN-DRIED CHERRY TOMATOES,
SHIITAKE MUSHROOMS & BROCCOLI RABE
  Frances Wilson, Lalime's 114

PEACH GALETTE
  Judith Maguire, Lalime's 115

CREAMED CORN & MARINATED TOMATOES WITH ASSORTED BASILS
  David Kinch, Restaurant Sent Sovi 116

WHITE PEACHES POACHED IN GEWÜRZTRAMINER WITH VANILLA & MASCARPONE
  Ralph Tingle, Bistro Ralph 117

SUMMER-FRUIT SHORTCAKES WITH LEMON CURD & WHIPPED CREAM
  Michael Quigley, Cafe Lolo 118

STUFFED CARAMELIZED TOMATOES WITH VANILLA ICE CREAM
  Paul Bertolli, Oliveto 120

CHICKEN POT PIE
  Dan Berman, Mixx 122

SUMMER MEDITERRANEAN GRATIN
  Gary Danko, Gary Danko 124

SUMMER SWEET CORN & YUKON GOLD CHOWDER WITH OKRA RELISH
  George Cronk, Park Grill 125

Summer Recipes

Corn Spoon Bread

SERVES 8

3 cups water

1 tablespoon salt

5 tablespoons butter

1 1/8 cups cornmeal

6 eggs, lightly beaten

1 1/4 cup buttermilk

3/8 cup cream

1 1/2 cups white sweet corn, cut from the cob

1. Preheat oven to 425°F.

2. Combine the water, salt, and butter in a heavy saucepan. Bring to a boil. Turn the heat down, and, stirring constantly, slowly pour in the cornmeal. Cook for 3 minutes, stirring vigorously.

3. Remove the pan from the heat, add the eggs and buttermilk, and mix well. Stir in the cream and corn and pour the batter into a lightly greased, 10x6-inch glass baking dish. Bake for 20 to 25 minutes.

Chef's Recommendation: Muscat, Albert Boxler 1997

Boulevard
San Francisco
Nancy Oakes
Chef/Owner

Late Summer Salad
Figs & Melon with Goat Cheese & Citrus Vinaigrette

SERVES 4

This lovely salad is on our menu at the end of summer, with autumn well on the way. Choose a flavorful melon—cantaloupe, Sharlyn, or Ambrosia—and the ripest fresh figs. We've chosen watercress for this salad, but delicate leaves of peppery arugula or red mustard greens are also delicious.

2 handfuls watercress, arugula, or red mustard greens

Citrus Vinaigrette (see sidebar)

1 small melon

8 to 10 ripe fresh figs; any combination of Kadota, Black Mission, or Calimyrna

2 ounces creamy, mild goat cheese, such as Redwood Hill chèvre

1. Sort through the watercress; trim the stems and discard bruised leaves. Wash the greens, dry in a spinner, wrap in a damp towel, and refrigerate. Make the vinaigrette.

2. Cut the melon in half and scoop out the seeds. Thinly slice and peel, keeping the contour of the melon.

3. Rinse the figs under cool water and pat dry. Cut in halves or quarters with the stem end intact.

4. Spread the watercress on a serving platter and arrange the melon and figs freely on top. Drizzle the vinaigrette over the fruit; crumble the goat cheese over all.

Chef's Recommendation: Chardonnay, such as those from Sonoma wineries like Sonoma Cutrer, Kent Rasmussen, and Clos du Bois

Menu note: Redwood Hill Farm in Sonoma County produces a number of delicious goat cheeses that are featured on the daily menu at Greens and on the Greens to Go take-out-counter menus.

Citrus Vinaigrette

makes ¹/₃ cup

¹/₄ teaspoon finely minced orange zest

2 tablespoons fresh orange juice

¹/₂ tablespoon champagne vinegar

¹/₄ teaspoon salt

3 tablespoons light olive oil

Combine everything but the oil in a small bowl. Then drizzle in the oil, whisking constantly.

greens

Greens
San Francisco
Annie Somerville
Executive Chef

**Cooking fresh
pod beans
and peas**

*Shell pod beans
and peas just
before cooking.
Boil about 2 cups
of water for every
¹/₂ cup of shelled
beans or peas; add
a dash of salt to
water, if desired.
Add beans or peas
to the boiling
water, stir,
quickly bring
back to boil, and
cook, uncovered,
until tender. Start
testing cranberry
beans for
tenderness at
30 minutes,
and black-eyed
peas at about
40 minutes.*

Rivoli
Berkeley
Wendy Brucker
Chef/Owner

Pan Roast Chicken Breasts
with Summer Succotash

SERVES 6

6 eight-ounce boneless chicken breasts with skin

Salt and pepper

1 tablespoon virgin olive oil

4 tablespoons diced onion

¹/₈ teaspoon paprika

¹/₂ cup fresh cranberry or kidney beans, cooked

¹/₂ cup fresh black-eyed peas, cooked

¹/₂ cup each: green and yellow beans, cooked and sliced diagonally
    into ¹/₂-inch pieces

1 cup corn kernels, cooked

2 tablespoons fresh thyme

2 cups chicken stock, reduced by half

3 tablespoons unsalted butter

1. Preheat oven to 450°F.

2. Season chicken with salt and pepper. Heat olive oil in a hot sauté pan
over medium heat. Add chicken breasts, skin side down, and cook for
6 to 7 minutes until the skin is brown and crispy. Place chicken in an
ovenproof dish, skin side up. Bake in oven 10 minutes or until juices run
clear—cooked through but juicy. Remove from dish and keep warm;
reserve pan juices.

3. Remove excess oil from sauté pan. Add the onion, paprika, cranberry
beans, black-eyed peas, beans, corn, thyme, chicken stock, and butter.
Bring to a simmer, stir gently, and cook until liquid is reduced by half.
Season with salt to taste. Set aside and keep warm.

4. To assemble, spoon succotash onto 6 dinner plates. Slice the chicken and
arrange over succotash. Pour reserved pan juices over chicken.

Chef's Recommendation: Chablis

Mediterranean Pasta

SERVES 2

12 medium Roma tomatoes

1 tablespoon virgin olive oil

4 large cloves garlic, minced

½ cup dry white wine

½ cup homemade vegetable stock or canned low-sodium chicken broth

¼ cup basil, finely sliced, across the veins, into ribbons, loosely packed

20 kalamata olives, pitted and slivered

3 ounces French feta cheese, crumbled

10 ounces fresh angel hair pasta, cooked al dente

Salt and freshly ground black pepper to taste

2 tablespoons Parmesan cheese, freshly grated

2 tablespoons pine nuts, lightly toasted

1. Peel and seed the tomatoes. To do this, have a pot of boiling water ready, score the stem end of each tomato with an X, and drop, 3 or 4 at a time, into the boiling water for 15 seconds. Remove with a slotted spoon and drop into a bowl of ice water for a few moments. Working over a bowl to catch their juice, peel the tomatoes with a paring knife, starting at the stem end; if the skin sticks, return to the boiling water for another 10 seconds. Cut the tomatoes in half—now with a sieve over the bowl—and gently scoop out the seeded pulp. Squeeze the pulp through the sieve and reserve the tomato juice. Cut the tomatoes into a fine dice.

2. In a large, hot sauté pan over medium flame, heat the olive oil. Add tomatoes, reserved juice, and garlic. Cook for 1 minute.

3. Add the wine and vegetable stock; deglaze by scraping the bottom of the pan and mixing well. Reduce by half, stirring frequently.

4. Add basil, kalamata olives, and feta cheese, and simmer for 1 minute. Add freshly cooked angel hair pasta. Toss to distribute ingredients. Season with salt and pepper to taste.

5. Divide between 2 warmed bowls. Top with Parmesan cheese and pine nuts.

Chef's Recommendation: Sangiovese il Fiasco, Bonny Doon

Bittersweet **Bistro**

Bittersweet
Bistro
Aptos
Thomas Vinolus
Chef/Proprietor

Arugula Salad
with Raw Sweet Corn & Sweet 100 Tomatoes

ALLOW PER PERSON:

1 dozen ripe sweet 100 tomatoes (Sungold orange ones are the sweetest)

1 small ear white corn with tiny, tender kernels

2 tablespoons extra virgin olive oil

A splash of white wine vinegar

A bit of freshly minced shallot

Sea salt and cracked black pepper

1 handful fresh arugula

1. Just before making the salad, wash the tomatoes and cut them in half. Husk the corn, rub off the silk, and slice off the kernels.

2. Combine the oil, vinegar, shallot, salt, and pepper together in a bowl and taste for seasoning. Use only a small amount of vinegar so that the sweetness of the vegetables defines the salad. Toss with the arugula to coat the leaves, and then add the tomatoes and the corn kernels.

3. If you have fresh nasturtiums in your garden, tear a few of them into this salad. The bright color and fragrant pepperiness are welcome in this summer salad.

Chef's Recommendation: rosé or fruity Friuli white wine

Zuni
San Francisco
Judy Rodgers
Chef/Owner

Baked Red Snapper
with Tomatoes, Peppers & Onions

SERVES 6

2 pounds red snapper fillets

1 1/2 teaspoons kosher salt

1/2 teaspoon fresh cracked black pepper

5 tablespoons olive oil

2 medium red onions, sliced

2 bell peppers (red, green, or yellow), sliced

1 teaspoon minced garlic

6 medium tomatoes, peeled, seeded, and cut in 1/2-inch strips

3 tablespoons chopped parsley

1/4 cup chopped fresh basil

Juice of 1 lemon

1. Preheat oven to 400°F.

2. Using needle-nose pliers, remove any bones that may remain in the fillets. Season the fish with 1 teaspoon of the salt and 1/4 teaspoon of the black pepper.

3. In a large skillet, heat 3 tablespoons of the olive oil over medium heat. Add the onions and cook until they have started to wilt, about 3 minutes. Add the peppers and continue cooking until they begin to soften, about 3 more minutes. Add the garlic and tomatoes. Lower the heat, cover, and cook for 5 minutes. Remove from heat and add the parsley, the basil, and the remaining 1/2 teaspoon of salt and 1/4 teaspoon of pepper.

4. Rub 1 tablespoon of the olive oil in a baking dish just large enough to hold the fish in one layer. Arrange the cooked vegetables in the bottom of the dish. Place the seasoned fish fillets on top. Sprinkle with lemon juice and the remaining tablespoon of olive oil.

5. Bake the fish in the preheated oven until it just flakes with a fork, about 10 to 15 minutes depending on the thickness of the fish. Check for doneness after 7 minutes. Serve the fish with the vegetables. Drizzle the juices from the baking dish over the top.

Chef's Recommendation: Sangiovese, Swanson, Napa

Lark Creek Inn
Larkspur
Bradley Ogden
Chef/Co-owner

Fresh Tuna Steak

12-ounce albacore tuna steak

2 teaspoons lemon juice

1 tablespoon olive oil

1/8 teaspoon salt

1/8 teaspoon pepper

Preheat the oven to 350°F. Place the tuna steak on a large square of foil. Brush both sides of the tuna with lemon juice and olive oil, and season with salt and pepper. Wrap tightly in foil and bake until cooked through; begin checking after 30 minutes. Cool the tuna steak and break it up into 2-inch flakes.

Flea Street Café
Menlo Park
Jesse Cool
Chef/Owner

Spicy Tuna, Caper, Anchovy & Tomato Sandwiches

SERVES 4

1 large can albacore tuna packed in water or cooked Fresh Tuna Steak (see sidebar)

1/4 cup finely minced red onion

1/2 cup finely chopped celery or fennel bulb

1 1/2 tablespoons capers

2 tablespoons chopped anchovy fillets

2 hard-boiled eggs, grated

2 tablespoons finely chopped parsley

3 tablespoons olive oil

1/2 teaspoon or more dried red chili flakes

8 slices bread

8 slices vine-ripened tomatoes

Salt and pepper, to taste

1. Drain off the water from the tuna. Combine the tuna with the red onion, celery, capers, anchovies, grated eggs, and parsley. Add enough olive oil to moisten thoroughly. Add chili flakes to taste, beginning with 1/2 teaspoon.

2. Lay out 4 pieces of bread and place 2 slices of tomato on each piece. Season with salt and pepper. Put a generous amount of tuna salad on top of the tomatoes. Top with the other piece of bread. Makes 4 sandwiches, with some tuna salad left over for lunch the next day!

Chef's Recommendation: beer or a merlot

Chopped Salad

SERVES 4

For the dressing:

1/4 cup Spanish olive brine (the liquid that olives are packed in)

2 tablespoons lemon juice

1/2 cup extra virgin olive oil

1/2 teaspoon freshly ground pepper

2 teaspoons chopped salt-packed anchovies

For the salad:

1 ripe tomato, diced

1/4 cup diced celery heart

1/4 cup diced English cucumber

1/4 cup diced fennel bulb

1/2 cup chopped Spanish olives

Salt to taste

1 head romaine lettuce, outer leaves discarded, ribs removed, and leaves torn into bite-size pieces

1/2 cup baby arugula

1/2 cup treviso or radicchio, chopped

1. Whisk together the olive brine, lemon juice, olive oil, pepper, and anchovies, and set aside at room temperature.

2. In a large salad bowl, combine the tomato, celery, cucumber, fennel, and olives. Toss with 1/2 cup of the dressing and a dash of salt. When the vegetables are thoroughly coated with the dressing, gently toss in the romaine, arugula, and treviso, and serve immediately.

Chef's Recommendation: El Toro Amber Ale

**Restaurant
LuLu**
San Francisco
Jody Denton
Chef/Partner

Corn Stock

Corn cobs (left over from pudding and White Truffle Butter)

Water to cover

Place corn cobs in a nonreactive pot, and cover with water. Simmer for 2 hours and strain.

Yellow Corn/Brioche Pudding
with White Truffle Butter

SERVES 6 TO 10

2 tablespoons butter

6 ounces leeks, cleaned and diced the same size as a kernel of corn

5 cups corn, cut off the cob (about 7 cobs; reserve cobs for Corn Stock)

1 teaspoon salt

4 cups Corn Stock (see sidebar)

Cream

4 eggs

6 additional egg yolks

1 tablespoon chopped thyme

White pepper to taste

4 cups brioche, diced to ⅓-inch cubes

White Truffle Butter (see sidebar on next page)

Chervil, chopped, for garnish

1. Preheat oven to 300°F.

2. In each of two separate pans, melt 1 tablespoon of the butter. Add the leeks to one pan and one cup of the corn to the other. Add ¼ teaspoon of the salt to each pan, and over low heat, gently sweat the leeks and corn until tender. Spread both out on a tray to cool.

3. In a covered, nonreactive pan, simmer the remaining corn, the Corn Stock, and a dash of salt until the corn is tender enough to puree, about 8 minutes. Puree the corn and corn stock in a blender and pass through a fine-mesh sieve. Add enough cream to make a total of 1 quart of liquid.

4. Whisk eggs and yolks to combine. Whisk in corn puree. Pass again through a fine-mesh sieve. Add leeks, corn, and thyme. Season with ½ teaspoon of the salt and white pepper.

restaurant
ELISABETH DANIEL

Elisabeth Daniel
San Francisco
Daniel Patterson
Chef/Owner

5. Combine this pudding mixture with brioche. Place equal amounts in 6 buttered 8-ounce ramekins or 1 large buttered, ovenproof baking dish. Place the ramekins or baking dish in a roasting pan and fill in halfway up the dishes with warm water to create a water bath. Cover with foil and bake until set. Remove and hold warm until serving.

6. Loosen puddings by running a thin knife around the inside of the molds, and unmold onto warm plates. Pour the White Truffle Butter over each one, and top with chervil.

Chef's Recommendation: Chardonnay, Rochioli Estate 1997

White Truffle Butter

Kernels cut from 6 ears of corn (reserve the cobs for the corn stock)

¹/₄ cup Corn Stock

6 tablespoons butter

2 tablespoons white truffle oil

Salt and white pepper to taste

Process the corn kernels through a juicer to produce about 1 cup of corn juice. Bring the corn juice to a boil in a small saucepan — it will start to thicken. Thin with the corn stock, turn the heat down to low, and whisk in the butter, one small piece at a time. Whisk in truffle oil and season to taste with salt and a pinch of white pepper.

Smoked Lamb & Garlic Sausage
with Roasted Red Pepper Confit & Mustard Sauce

SERVES 4

For the Red Pepper Confit:

$^1/_2$ small red onion, peeled and julienned

$^1/_2$ red bell pepper, ends cut off, seeds and core removed, and julienned

$^1/_2$ yellow bell pepper, ends cut off, seeds and core removed, and julienned

$^1/_2$ green bell pepper, ends cut off, seeds and core removed, and julienned

2 creamer (new) potatoes, julienned

1 tablespoon extra virgin olive oil

$^1/_2$ tablespoon sherry wine vinegar

1 teaspoon fresh thyme leaves, chopped fine

Salt and pepper to taste

For the Sweet and Sour Mustard Sauce:

$^1/_2$ cup Coleman's dry mustard

1 cup rice vinegar

$1^1/_2$ tablespoon yellow miso

$^3/_4$ cup sugar

3 eggs

$^1/_2$ cup whole-grain mustard

Salt and pepper to taste

To assemble:

1 pound Gingrass Family Smoked Lamb and Garlic Sausage or other
   handmade smoked sausage

Deep-Fried Potato Sticks to garnish (see next page)

1. To make the confit, sauté the onion, peppers, and potatoes in the olive
   oil until caramelized. Deglaze with the vinegar. Then add the thyme, and
   season with salt and pepper. Set aside.

2. To make the mustard sauce, combine the dry mustard, rice vinegar,
   miso, sugar, and eggs in a double boiler and whisk over heat until the
   mixture becomes thick. Strain into a bowl through a fine strainer and

**Hawthorne
Lane**
San Francisco
Anne Gingrass
Executive Chef/
Proprietor

allow to cool. Whisk in the whole-grain mustard and season with salt and pepper. Set aside.

3. Light the grill. Grill the sausages over high heat until they are deep brown in color and have a crispy skin. Remove from the grill and slice into slices.

4. On 4 dinner plates, arrange one-quarter of the slices around each plate and drizzle with the mustard sauce. Place about one-quarter of the confit in the center of each plate and garnish with Deep-Fried Potato Sticks.

Chef's Recommendation: Zinfandel

Deep-Fried Potato Sticks

1¹/₂ pounds baking potatoes

Vegetable oil for frying

Salt

Pepper

1. Peel the potatoes and cut them into shoestrings, using a sharp knife or French mandoline. Put the potatoes in a bowl of cold water and soak for 10 minutes.

2. In a large, heavy pot, heat oil to 340°F.

3. Dry the potatoes thoroughly and fry for 3 to 7 minutes until they are cooked but not brown. Drain them and reserve.

4. Raise the heat of the oil to 390°F. Test the oil by dropping in a piece of bread. It should brown in 30 seconds. Put the potatoes back in the oil and fry until they are brown. Drain and keep warm in a 300°F oven. Do not add salt until you are ready to serve or they will become soggy.

Zinfandel Vinaigrette

yield: 2 cups

²/₃ cup zinfandel vinegar or a good-quality red wine vinegar

1¹/₃ cups virgin olive oil

2 tablespoons minced shallot

1 teaspoon salt

¹/₂ teaspoon black pepper

Combine all of the ingredients together in a small bowl and whisk until fully incorporated. Store, refrigerated, in a glass jar with a tight-fitting lid for up to 2 weeks.

Grilled Fish
with Heirloom Tomatoes & Salsa Verde

SERVES 4

4 heirloom tomatoes

¹/₄ cup Zinfandel Vinaigrette (see sidebar)

1 small mackerel or 4 whole fresh sardine fillets (or an appropriate amount of other small fresh fish)

2 tablespoons virgin olive oil

1 teaspoon salt

¹/₂ teaspoon black pepper

1 tablespoon Salsa Verde (see next page)

1. Preheat gas or charcoal grill to medium hot.

2. Slice the tomatoes and combine them in a small bowl with the vinaigrette. Gently toss the tomatoes until thoroughly coated with the dressing. Allow the tomatoes to marinate for at least 10 minutes.

3. Coat the fish with olive oil and season with salt and pepper. Gently place the seasoned fish on the grill and cook it for about 3 minutes on each side or until the flesh begins to flake and pull away from the bone easily.

4. Arrange the marinated tomatoes on a small oval plate and rest the grilled fish on top. Drizzle the fish with Salsa Verde and serve immediately.

Chef's Recommendation: Vermentino, Il Monticello 1997

Rose Pistola

Rose Pistola
San Francisco
Reed Hearon
Chef/Owner

Salsa Verde

yield: approximately 1 cup

¹/₄ bunch basil

¹/₄ bunch Italian parsley

¹/₂ cup Zinfandel Vinaigrette (see sidebar)

¹/₂ slice day-old bread, broken into small pieces

1 tablespoon capers, rinsed twice and drained thoroughly

¹/₂ tablespoon chopped garlic

¹/₄ teaspoon cracked black pepper

2 small, canned anchovy fillets

Wash and pat dry the basil and parsley. Remove the leaves from the stems and discard the stems. Combine the vinaigrette and the bread pieces in a small bowl, and let rest for 15 minutes.

In a food processor or blender, combine the basil and parsley, the bread-and-vinaigrette mixture, and the capers, garlic, black pepper, and anchovy fillets. Puree the salsa until thoroughly combined and very smooth. Salsa Verde may be stored under refrigeration for 2 days.

**Local Foods
Local Flavors**

Niman Ranch *supplies gourmet-quality beef, pork, and lamb to San Francisco Bay Area restaurants and fine markets. In contrast to the mass production of meat on so-called modern factory farms, Niman Ranch has developed a network of sustainable family farms owned by ranchers who, by agreement, raise their animals free range on grass and natural feeds — without steroids, subtherapeutic antibiotics, or other artificial growth promotants —and who treat their animals with dignity and respect.*

A great summer
dessert. Use any
red-fleshed plum
or plucots from
the farmers
market. Serve
warm with Rice
Dream or coconut
sorbet.

Ginger-Glazed Plum & Walnut Galette

YIELDS 6 TO 8 GALETTES

$^1/_2$ cup walnuts

3 cups white flour, unbleached

$^1/_4$ cup Sucanat

1 teaspoon sea salt

$^1/_4$ teaspoon black pepper

$^3/_4$ cup canola oil

1 teaspoon vanilla

$^1/_2$ cup soy milk

4 red-fleshed plums, sliced thin

Sugar-Ginger Glaze (see sidebar on next page)

Rice Dream or coconut sorbet

1. Preheat oven to 350°F.

2. Place the walnuts on a cookie sheet, and toast in the oven for 10 to 15 minutes. Remove the walnuts from the oven, cool, and dice by hand or in a food processor.

3. Sift the flour into a bowl and whisk in the diced nuts, Sucanat, salt, and black pepper. Drizzle the oil over the dry ingredients, covering as much surface area as possible. Mix lightly with a spatula until the flour and oil form little balls.

4. Combine the vanilla and soy milk and add to the dough. Mix until a ball is formed. If the mixture appears to be dry and doesn't come together, add more soy milk, 1 tablespoon at a time, until the mixture holds together. Wrap the ball in plastic wrap and refrigerate until well chilled.

5. To assemble and bake, preheat oven to 350°F.

6. Take the pastry dough out of the refrigerator. Keeping the reserved dough well wrapped, take $^1/_7$ of the dough. Roll it out between two sheets of parchment or waxed paper to form a circle that is slightly larger than 6 inches in diameter. Carefully remove the top piece of parchment, and re-place it lightly on the surface of the dough. Flip the dough and remove the top piece of parchment.

Millennium
San Francisco
Eric Tucker
Head Chef

7. With a paring knife, cut the dough into a circle that is roughly 5$\frac{1}{2}$ inches in diameter (a small plate can be used as a guide). Remove the excess dough. Place about half a plum's worth of slices in the center of the dough. Brush the plums with Sugar-Ginger Glaze. Fold the sides of the circle over the filling—leaving the center open—to create a galette that is a rough square.

8. Place the galette on a parchment-lined cookie sheet. Repeat with the rest of the dough and the plums.

9. When all of the galettes have been made, bake them for 35 minutes or until crusts are golden brown and the plums are lightly caramelized. Remove from the oven and cool on a rack. Serve the galettes warm, with Rice Dream or coconut sorbet. They may be rewarmed.

Chef's Recommendation: tawny port

Sugar-Ginger Glaze

4 tablespoons unrefined sugar

$\frac{1}{2}$ cup water

2 tablespoons grated fresh ginger

In a small saucepan, heat the sugar and water to boiling. Reduce the heat and simmer until slightly thick-ened, about 1 to 2 minutes. Remove from heat and add the ginger.

To blanch broccoli rabe

Bring a pot of water to a boil and blanch the broccoli rabe in the boiling water for about 3 minutes. Drain and set to one side.

Roasted Salmon
with Oven-Dried Cherry Tomatoes, Shiitake Mushrooms & Broccoli Rabe

SERVES 4

1 basket cherry tomatoes

5 tablespoons olive oil plus a little to drizzle over fish

1 tablespoon lemon juice plus a little to drizzle over fish

2 cloves garlic, finely minced

Salt and pepper to taste

4 five-ounce portions of salmon fillet

1 pound fresh saffron fettuccine

1 pound shiitake mushrooms, cleaned and coarsely chopped

2 bunches broccoli rabe (about 1½ pounds), washed, trimmed, coarsely chopped, and blanched (see sidebar)

1. Preheat oven to 250°F.

2. Wash and cut the cherry tomatoes in half. Toss them in 2 tablespoons of the olive oil, 1 tablespoon of the lemon juice, one clove of the garlic, salt, and pepper. Lay them out on a cookie sheet and place them in the oven for about an hour, until the tomatoes have dried but still remain soft. This can be done several days in advance and kept refrigerated.

3. Reheat or reset the oven to 400°F. Place the salmon fillets on a greased ovenproof dish and season with salt and pepper. Drizzle with some olive oil and lemon juice. Roast the salmon in the oven until cooked through, 10 to 18 minutes depending on the thickness. Begin checking after 10 minutes so the fish doesn't overcook.

4. Bring 4 quarts of water to a boil and add 1 tablespoon of salt. Put the pasta in the water, cover, and bring back to a boil. Remove the cover and cook for 3 minutes or until done. Drain well.

5. Heat 1 tablespoon of the olive oil. Add 1 clove of the garlic and the shiitake mushrooms. Sauté until the mushrooms are soft. Add the oven-dried tomatoes and the broccoli rabe and toss well. Add the hot drained pasta and toss with 2 tablespoons of the olive oil, salt, and pepper. Divide the pasta among 4 plates. Place the roasted salmon on top and serve.

Chef's Recommendation: Le Cigare Volant, Bonny Doon, Santa Cruz 1996

Lalime's
Berkeley
Frances Wilson
Executive Chef

Peach Galette

SERVES 8

For the crust:

2 cups all-purpose flour

1/2 teaspoon salt

1 1/2 teaspoons sugar

8 ounces (two sticks) cold sweet butter, cut into pieces

1/3 cup cold whole milk

1 tablespoon cider vinegar

For the filling:

6 peaches, peeled and cut into 1/4-inch slices

2 tablespoons all-purpose flour

1/4 cup sugar

1/4 teaspoon cinnamon

1/4 teaspoon freshly grated nutmeg

1. Blend flour, salt, and sugar in a bowl. With a pastry blender, cut butter into flour, scraping off and incorporating the butter clinging to the blender; cut until mixture resembles coarse meal. Add milk to vinegar, stir briskly, and sprinkle over flour mixture. Work the liquid into the mixture by running your fingers down the inside and around the bottom of the bowl, turning and lifting until the mixture forms a ball of dough. On a lightly floured surface, gently press the ball into a flat disk, and roll it until it's 1/4-inch thick; trim into a 14-inch circle, using a plate to guide you. Prick the pastry in several places with a fork. While preparing filling, chill the formed pastry in the refrigerator on a cookie sheet lined with parchment.

2. To prepare the filling, peel and cut the peaches over a bowl to catch their juice. In a small bowl, mix flour, sugar, cinnamon, and nutmeg. Add to peaches and toss carefully until peaches are fully coated.

3. Spoon peach mixture into the center of the dough circle. Fold edges up to partially enclose filling. Chill in the refrigerator for 1 hour.

4. Preheat oven to 375°F. Bake the galette for 35 to 40 minutes, until crisp and golden brown. Cool on rack. Serve warm or at room temperature.

Chef's Recommendation: White Riesling, Navarro Cluster Select, Anderson Valley 1997

Lalime's
Berkeley
Judith Maguire
Pastry Chef

Creamed Corn & Marinated Tomatoes
with Assorted Basils

SERVES 5 TO 8

1½ cups heavy cream

2 pounds assorted heirloom tomatoes

2 bunches different types of basil

2 shallots, minced

1 teaspoon salt

½ teaspoon black pepper

1 tablespoon red wine vinegar

3 tablespoons virgin olive oil

Kernels cut from 5 ears of corn

1. Place the cream in a heavy saucepan and bring it to a boil over medium-high heat. Continue to boil until it has reduced in volume by half and has thickened. While the cream is reducing, cut the tomatoes into interesting angles and shapes and arrange them on a tray or platter.

2. Pick all of the beautiful tops off the basil and set them aside. Take the larger leaves and cut them into a fine chiffonade (thin strips). Sprinkle the tomatoes with shallots, basil chiffonade, ½ teaspoon of the salt, ¼ teaspoon of the pepper, and a drizzle of red wine vinegar and virgin olive oil.

3. Add the corn to the thickened cream. Stir and bring to a simmer. Season with salt and pepper.

4. Arrange the tomatoes on dinner plates, with an emphasis on variety in shapes and colors. Just before serving, spoon some of the creamed corn on top of the tomatoes and garnish with the basil sprigs. Serve immediately to contrast the warmth of the corn and the coolness of the tomatoes.

Chef's Recommendation: Chardonnay McGregor, Mount Eden Vineyards, Edna Valley 1997

Restaurant Sent Sovi
Saratoga
David Kinch
Chef/Owner

White Peaches Poached in Gewürztraminer
with Vanilla & Mascarpone

SERVES 6

6 large white peaches, peeled: nectar is the best variety; try to find fruit
  that is firm, yet ripe (see sidebar)

1 vanilla bean (Tahitian, if possible)

1 bottle dry Gewürztraminer

1 cinnamon stick

3 whole cloves

1 pinch freshly ground nutmeg

3/4 cup sugar

6 tablespoons mascarpone, at room temperature

6 mint sprigs, optional

Cookies, optional

1. Peel the peaches according to the instructions in the sidebar.

2. Slice the vanilla bean down the middle so it releases not only the flavor
   but also the tiny black seeds inside. To prepare the poaching liquid,
   discard the boiled water used to peel the peaches, and, using the same
   pot, combine the Gewürztraminer, cinnamon, cloves, nutmeg, and split
   vanilla bean. Add the sugar, and if your Gewürztraminer is not dry, use
   less sugar. Mix well, stirring until the sugar dissolves. Submerge the
   peaches in the poaching liquid; add water to cover, if necessary. Poach
   over low to medium heat for about 25 minutes depending on the ripeness of the peaches. When the peaches are soft enough to eat easily with
   a dessert spoon, remove them carefully from the poaching liquid with
   a slotted spoon. Place on a large, flat platter to cool.

3. To create a sauce for the peaches, boil the poaching liquid over medium-
   high heat until reduced by half.

4. When the peaches have cooled, work from the stem ends and carefully
   dig out the pits with a paring knife. Be cautious not to tear apart the
   peaches while removing their pits. Removing the pit will form a pocket.
   Fill each pocket with 1 tablespoon of the mascarpone.

5. Place the filled peaches in dessert bowls, pocket sides down. Pour some
   of the thickened poaching liquid over them and serve at room temperature. Fresh mint sprigs work well as garnishes, along with your choice
   of cookies. *Chef's Recommendation: champagne or Vin Santo*

*Bring a large pot
of water to a boil.
Using a paring
knife, lightly
score an X on the
stem end of each
peach. Drop the
peaches, 2 or 3 at
a time, into the
rapidly boiling
water for 15
seconds. Remove
them immediately
and gently put
them in a deep
bowl with ice
water to cover.
When cool
enough to handle,
gently pull the
skin from the
fruit with a
paring knife.
The skin should
slip right off.*

Bistro Ralph
Healdsburg
Ralph Tingle
Chef/Owner

Lemon Curd

5¼ teaspoons lemon zest, finely grated

¾ cup plus 2 tablespoons fresh lemon juice

6 eggs, beaten until pale yellow

1¼ cups sugar

10 tablespoons melted sweet butter

In a heavy, nonreactive saucepan, combine all ingredients, and, stirring frequently, cook over low heat until thick. Strain and cool. Note: It's not necessary to use a double boiler.

Cafe Lolo
Santa Rosa
Michael Quigley
Chef/Owner

Summer-Fruit Shortcakes
with Lemon Curd & Whipped Cream

SERVES 8

For the shortcakes:

2 cups all-purpose flour

1 tablespoon baking powder

½ teaspoon salt

⅓ cup sugar

½ cup cold sweet butter, cut into small chunks

1 egg, lightly beaten

½ cup cold heavy cream

Melted sweet butter

Sugar for topping

To assemble:

6 cups assorted, fresh seasonal fruits, cut into bite-size slices

4 tablespoons sugar

1 cup Lemon Curd (see sidebar)

½ cup heavy cream, whipped

Powdered sugar, sifted once

1. Preheat oven to 350°F.

2. Using your fingers, quickly and gently combine flour, baking powder, salt, sugar, and butter. As you work, incorporate all ingredients from sides and bottom of bowl, but work only until dough is the consistency of coarse cornmeal. Do not overmix. Add the egg and the cream, and mix well to form dough. Chill in refrigerator for 30 minutes.

3. On a lightly floured board, roll the dough into a 1½-inch-thick square. (If you prefer to spread the dough with your hands, dip your fingers into cold water to prevent the dough from sticking to you.) Carefully fold dough in half, place on a buttered cookie sheet dusted with flour, and unfold to full length. Cut the dough into 8 squares. Separate the squares, brush with the melted butter, and sprinkle with sugar. Bake for 25 minutes or until a light golden brown.

4. Place sliced fruit in a mixing bowl and toss gently with sugar until well coated. Let stand 20 minutes.

5. Cut shortcake squares in half; for the base of the shortcake, place one half on the individual dessert plates. Place equal amounts of fruit over each shortcake base, drizzle with lemon curd, and then spoon a dollop of whipped cream over all. Finish with the second half of the shortcake square arranged at an angle on top of the whipped cream. Dust plate with powdered sugar and serve.

Chef's Recommendation: Chappelet

**Local Foods
Local Flavors**

Bellwether Farms *started California's first sheep dairy in 1990. A family-owned and -operated farm in Sonoma County, the farm specializes in producing delicious cheeses by using traditional methods.*
In addition to sheep milk cheeses, Bellwether Farms makes cheese using pure Jersey Cow milk. Its award-winning cheeses are truly special.

Stuffed Caramelized Tomatoes
with Vanilla Ice Cream

SERVES 6

12 small tomatoes

2 ripe but firm pears, peeled and finely diced

2 slices fresh pineapple, finely diced

2 green apples, peeled and finely diced

1 vanilla bean

1 tablespoon pistachio nuts, coarsely chopped

1 tablespoon walnuts, coarsely chopped

1 tablespoon peeled almonds, coarsely chopped

$1^1/_3$ cups granulated sugar

Grated zest of 1 lemon

Grated zest of $^1/_2$ orange

1 tablespoon grated fresh ginger

$^1/_8$ teaspoon ground clove

Pinch of cinnamon

Pinch of ground anise

$^1/_4$ cup fresh mint leaves, chopped

$2^1/_2$ cups orange juice, fresh squeezed from about 10 oranges

3 cups vanilla ice cream

1. Preheat oven to 375°F.

2. To peel the tomatoes, drop them into boiling water for 15 seconds, remove them, and dip them into ice water. Peel off the skins and cut a slice from the top to form a hat. Use a small spoon to remove the pulp from the inside of each tomato. Reserve the pulp.

3. In a bowl, combine the diced pears, pineapple, and apples. Split the vanilla bean lengthwise and scrape the contents of the bean into the bowl. Add the pistachio nuts, walnuts, and almonds.

Oliveto

Oliveto
Oakland
Paul Bertolli
Chef/Owner

4. Pour ⅓ cup of the sugar into a sauté pan and add a tablespoon of water. Stir, place over high heat, and allow the sugar to melt for about 1 minute. Add the fruit-and-nut mixture. Cook for 5 to 7 minutes, until the fruits soften slightly.

5. Remove from the heat. Add the lemon and orange zests, reserved tomato pulp, grated ginger, cloves, cinnamon, anise, and mint leaves. Mix well, fill the tomatoes, and top with their hats.

6. Place 1 cup of the sugar and ¼ cup of water in an ovenproof casserole that is just large enough to hold the tomatoes side by side. Place over high heat and cook until the sugar turns golden brown. Do not allow the sugar to cook beyond caramel color. If it gets too dark, remove it from the heat and start again. (Note: Sugar this hot can be very dangerous, so handle it carefully. Use boiling water to remove it from spoons and pans and keep a bowl of ice water nearby in case of burns). Add the orange juice very slowly to the caramel, stirring constantly. (Be very careful because the caramel can foam and boil over.) Bring the orange juice and caramel to a boil, making sure all of the sugar has melted. Boil until the mixture has thickened slightly, about 10 minutes. Remove from the heat.

7. Place the tomatoes in the casserole. Bake for 8 minutes. Remove from the oven. As the tomatoes cool, baste them frequently with the caramelized orange sauce. Serve the tomatoes while still slightly warm. Serve two on a plate in a pool of caramel orange sauce with a scoop of vanilla ice cream.

To parboil vegetables

Drop prepared vegetables in rapidly boiling water for about 1 to 2 minutes each, until tender crisp. Remove immediately and plunge into ice water to stop cooking. Parboil the carrots, the two beans, the broccoli, and the cauliflower separately.

Chicken Pot Pie

SERVES 2

2 five-inch-square pieces puff pastry

1 egg, lightly beaten for egg wash

8 to 10 ounces boneless chicken breast, cut into $1/2$-inch cubes

Salt and freshly ground black pepper to taste

$1/2$ cup flour

2 tablespoons virgin olive oil

$1/2$ cup Marsala

$3/4$ cup chicken stock, reduced by half

$1/2$ cup heavy cream

$1/2$ teaspoon fresh thyme, chopped

$1/2$ teaspoon fresh rosemary, finely minced

2 tablespoons unsalted butter

3 to 4 ounces cremini mushrooms, thinly sliced

1 tablespoon finely chopped shallot

2 ounces red or green (or both) chard, removed from stem, washed, and cut into ribbons

8 baby carrots, cut diagonally into $1/2$-inch coins, parboiled al dente

8 green beans, cut diagonally into $1/2$-inch slices, parboiled al dente

8 yellow beans, cut diagonally into $1/2$-inch slices, parboiled al dente

8 bite-size broccoli florets, parboiled al dente

8 bite-size cauliflower florets, parboiled al dente

1. Preheat oven to 350°F.

2. Place the puff pastry squares on a cookie sheet—do not crowd—and brush with the egg wash. Bake 12 to 15 minutes, completely rotate sheet on oven shelf, and bake another 12 to 15 minutes or until golden brown. Set aside.

3. Season cubed chicken with salt and pepper to taste, dredge in flour, and shake off excess. Heat the olive oil in a hot sauté pan over medium heat. When hot, add chicken and brown on all sides. Add the Marsala, shake

Mixx
Santa Rosa
Dan Berman
Chef/Proprietor

the pan, and stir while scraping up all bits from the bottom of the pan. Reduce by half, add the chicken stock, and stir well. Lower heat and slowly add cream, stirring well and constantly. Reduce until sauce just evenly coats the back of a spoon. Remove from heat. Add thyme and rosemary and season with salt and pepper to taste.

4. In another pan, melt 1 tablespoon of the unsalted butter, add mushrooms, and sauté about 2 minutes. Add shallots and chard, stir well, and cook 1 to 2 minutes more.

5. Reheat the parboiled vegetables by dropping the carrots, beans, broccoli, and cauliflower into a pot of almost boiling water for about 30 seconds. Remove and place in a stainless steel bowl with the remaining 1 tablespoon of the butter, toss until coated, and season with salt and pepper to taste.

6. To serve, warm 2 dinner plates. Cut each pastry square in half horizontally. Place 1 puff pastry square—the bottom—on each plate. Arrange vegetables alternately along the inner edges of the square, creating small mounds of each vegetable on each square.

7. Heat the chicken and sauce and adjust the seasoning. With a large serving spoon, evenly distribute the chicken and sauce in the center of each pastry-bottom square. Pour remaining sauce over vegetables and around pastry. Place the second square of pastry at a slight angle on the chicken mixture. Top with the chard-and-mushroom mixture. Serve immediately.

Chef's Recommendation: Estate Sauvignon Blanc, Rochioli, Russian River Valley 1998

**Local Foods
Local Flavors**

*Rocky the Range Chicken was created in 1986, when several California superstar chefs challenged Petaluma Poultry Processors to produce a flavorful free-range chicken in the United States equal to those found in Europe. The result is a chicken nourished by an all-natural vegetarian diet containing no antibiotics, animal by-products, or additives and raised under humane, stress-reducing methods. Petaluma Poultry Processors also produces **Rosie the Organic Chicken**—a certified organic chicken raised on 100 percent organic feed.*

Summer Mediterranean Gratin

SERVES 4

1¹/₂ pounds eggplant, sliced ¹/₂-inch thick

¹/₂ cup light olive oil

1¹/₂ pounds zucchini, sliced into ¹/₄-inch rounds

3 medium onions, peeled and coarsely minced

1¹/₂ pounds fennel bulb, sliced ¹/₈-inch thick

¹/₂ cup fine fresh bread crumbs

1 cup grated Parmigiano-Reggiano

4 tablespoons fresh basil leaves, coarsely chopped

4 tablespoons Italian flat-leaf parsley, finely chopped

1 tablespoon fresh thyme leaves, coarsely chopped

4 tablespoons scallions, green parts only, or chives, finely chopped

Salt and freshly ground black pepper

1¹/₂ pounds large ripe tomatoes, sliced ¹/₄-inch thick

1. Preheat oven to 450°F.

2. Place eggplant slices on a thick sheet pan. Brush both sides of the eggplant with a thin coat of olive oil. Bake for 10 to 15 minutes or until golden brown. Remove from oven and cool.

3. In a large, hot sauté pan, heat 3 tablespoons of the olive oil over a medium-high flame, add the zucchini slices, turn heat to high, and sauté for 4 minutes. Salt lightly. Remove from pan and cool.

4. Using the same sauté pan, heat 3 tablespoons of the olive oil, stir in the onion, and sauté for 4 minutes. Add the fennel and cook until tender, over low heat, about 30 minutes. Salt to taste. Let cool.

5. In a bowl, combine the bread crumbs, cheese, herbs, scallions or chives, 1 teaspoon salt (or to taste), and several grinds of pepper.

6. Reduce oven to 350°F. Lightly brush a 16x10-inch gratin dish with olive oil. Line the bottom of the dish with half the onion-fennel mixture, and in succession, cover with a layer of sliced tomatoes, a layer of zucchini, and a layer of eggplant. Between each layer, sprinkle ¹/₄ cup of the bread-crumb-grated cheese mixture. Repeat, using all the vegetables and ending with a layer of eggplant. Bake for 50 to 70 minutes, until bubbly and slightly brown on top. Serve warm or at room temperature. The gratin is best if allowed to mellow at least ¹/₂ hour before serving. It also reheats well.
Chef's Recommendation: Rosato of Sangiovese, Swanson Vineyards, Napa

GARY DANKO

Gary Danko
San Francisco
Gary Danko
Chef/Owner

Summer Sweet Corn & Yukon Gold Chowder
with Okra Relish

SERVES 8

4 tablespoons butter

1 tablespoon diced garlic

2 tablespoons diced shallots

$^1/_2$ onion, diced

$^1/_2$ leek, diced

1 stalk celery, diced

8 ears corn, kernels removed from the cob

2 cups white wine

2 quarts chicken stock

Salt and pepper to taste

2 pounds Yukon Gold potatoes, diced

$^1/_2$ quart heavy cream

2 tablespoons snipped chives

Okra Relish (see sidebar)

1. In a soup pot, melt butter over low heat. Add garlic, shallots, onion, leek, celery, and corn kernels and cook over low heat until the vegetables are softened but not browned. Pour white wine over the vegetables. Stir in the wine and reduce by boiling rapidly for 6 minutes.

2. Add chicken stock and cook until vegetables are tender and the soup has good flavor. Check seasoning and add salt and pepper, if necessary. Add potatoes and cook until tender. Finish by adding the cream and chives.

3. Ladle soup into bowls, season with salt and pepper, and garnish with Okra Relish.

Chef's Recommendation: Caymus Conundrum 1996

Okra Relish

$^1/_2$ pound fresh okra, sliced

$^1/_2$ pound Roma tomatoes, peeled and diced

$1^1/_2$ ounces lemon juice

$^1/_2$ cup olive oil

1 tablespoon or more basil chiffonade (thin strips) to taste

Combine all ingredients.

□□ **PARK GRILL** □□

**Park Hyatt
San Francisco**
San Francisco
George Cronk
Former Executive
Chef

eNJOYING THE HARVEST AND

ENSURING CONTINUED ABUNDANCE

BAY AREA FALL CROPS

ALMONDS
APPLES
ARTICHOKES
ARUGULA
BEETS
BROCCOLI
CABBAGES
CARROTS
CAULIFLOWER
CELERY ROOT
CEPES
CHANTERELLES
CHARD
CHESTNUTS
CIPPOLINI ONIONS
CRANBERRIES
DIAKON RADISHES
ESCAROLE
FENNEL
FIGS
FRISEE
GRAPES
GREEN BEANS
HUCKLEBERRIES
KALE
KIWI
LEEKS
LEMONS

LETTUCES
MACHE
MINER'S LETTUCE
MIZUNA
MUSTARD GREENS
PARSNIPS
PEARS
PEPPERS
PERSIMMONS
POMEGRANATES
POTATOES
PUMPKINS
QUINCE
RADICCHIO
RADISHES
RASPBERRIES
ROMAINE
RUTABAGAS
SATSUMA MANDARINS
SHALLOTS
SHELL BEANS
SPINACH
SWEET POTATOES
TANGERINES
TURNIPS
WALNUTS
WILD MUSHROOMS
WINTER SQUASHES

By the time October rolls around, we have been harvesting almost every day for more than six months. We're tired, and starting to dream about taking it easy for a few months during the winter. As we finish harvesting each block of strawberries or vegetables, we plant a cover crop—a grain-and-legume mix that will grow throughout the winter, improving the soil and protecting it from the winter cold and rains. When we disc up the last block of strawberries in November, nobody sheds a tear.

Farming in the Fall

All summer long we've been preparing a new piece of ground for the planting of new strawberry transplants. By September we've made the beds and are letting the soil rest before introducing the new plants. We plant into fragrant soil. Optimism is in the air: these new plants will produce beautiful fruit by the following April.

The first leaves appear on the new plants in November. Their bright-green color is so hopeful! We watch every new leaf appear. Very soon the weeds appear as well. All of our brilliant ideas about how to reduce their numbers have come to naught, and we have just as many weeds as last year. We are destined to spend the next few months keeping them down so the new plants can thrive. We hope for dry spells between the rains so the weeds don't get out of hand.

By the end of November, most of the crops are harvested, the new strawberries are planted, and the cover crops are growing. We've done our part.

Many times during the season, we have been reminded of our humble place in the grand scheme of things. With the celebration of Thanksgiving, we take the time to look up—and all around us—and formally declare our humility before the wonder of it all.

By mid-December, everything is tidied up and we're ready for some relaxed time with family and friends during the holidays. Our work for the year is done. We decide to wait until January to make the inevitable appointment with our accountant.

Along the Pacific coast south of San Francisco and north of Santa Cruz is Swanton Berry Farm, a certified organic grower specializing in strawberries. Swanton Berry Farm's concern for the environment has led to a long-term soil-building program as well as regular crop rotation. Swanton Berry is the first strawberry farm—and the first organic farm—in the United States to sign a contract with the United Farmworkers of America/AFL-CIO in an effort to present customers with products that are not produced at the expense of workers' health or dignity.

by Jim Cochran
Swanton Berry
Farm
Davenport,
California

> *"Acre by acre, California's best farmland is being paved over by suburban sprawl. This kind of rapid, ill-planned development is costly—agriculturally, economically, environmentally, and socially."*
>
> *— Terry Wetzel, California field director of the American Farmland Trust*

Saving the Land that Feeds America

The conversion of California's farmland into suburban sprawl is the single most critical natural resource and public policy issue confronting the state today. In its 1997 Farming on the Edge report, American Farmland Trust identified California's Sacramento and San Joaquin valleys, which together form the Central Valley, as the most threatened agricultural region in the United States. Without equal in the United States, the Central Valley region produces more than $16 billion worth of farm products each year— roughly two-thirds of California's farm production.

Unfortunately, what's happening in California is happening in many areas of the country. The best and most productive farmland is under constant threat of development. In fact, according to the U.S. Department of Agriculture, the land most likely to be converted to nonagricultural uses is prime farmland. The reason is simple: years ago agriculture was the basis for permanent settlement, and the country's settlers were understandably drawn to the most fertile land. Those early settlements have grown into highly populated urban centers rimmed by thriving suburbs. And as those communities grow, the rich, productive land that surrounds them becomes the prime target for development.

No issue will be more important in 21st-century America than how we use our dwindling land resources. The competition for land—especially productive farm and ranch land—will intensify as both the population grows and communications technology makes it easier to live and work in widely dispersed communities. For instance, if you live in the San Francisco Bay Area, you've most likely seen the effects of suburban sprawl and its encroachment on open space. So the question is, What do communities blessed with some of the world's finest agriculture need to know about preserving farmland?

Why Save Farms?

by Bernadine Prince
Director
Public Education
American
Farmland Trust

Saving farmland is an investment in your community. Not only is farmland of immense value in terms of the food and fiber it produces and the jobs it supports; it also helps maintain a community's economic stability. Privately owned open lands generate more in tax revenues than they require in municipal services. Pastoral landscapes attract tourists and provide scenic beauty and open spaces. And agriculture contributes to a state's economy not only through jobs, sales, and support services but also by supplying lucrative secondary markets such as food processing.

Equally important are the environmental benefits. Well-managed farms can contribute to wildlife habitats and can act as a buffer between urban and wilderness areas. Furthermore, by protecting the most productive farmland, we reduce the pressure for intensive agricultural use of lands that are less productive: farming on poorer-quality land, which can result in increased soil erosion, water pollution, wetlands drainage problems, and greater use of fertilizers and pesticides.

How Can You Help Protect Farmland?

Efforts to protect America's farmland begin at the local level, where sprawl threatens community character and endangers fiscal stability. Two important—and simple—ways you can help save farmland in your region are to buy locally grown foods and to support the stores and restaurants that offer the products of local farms.

Responsible local planning is also needed to ensure the future of our prime farmland. Americans must recognize that irrevocable decisions regarding the fate of farmland are being made every day without guidance from us, the voting public. To have a true impact on preserving farmland, your community must join together to establish a viable plan that will contain sprawl and promote farming in increasingly diverse communities.

Rich, productive farmland is one of the most valuable assets this country possesses. And it is—and should remain—an integral part of California's Bay Area and central coast communities. Farmland is an investment that pays off in better quality of life for everyone. We must be thoughtful and strategic in our approach to protecting farmland so that it may continue to be a source of renewable wealth that no nation can challenge.

American Farmland Trust

The **American Farmland Trust (AFT)** is a private, nonprofit organization founded in 1980 to protect farmland in the United States. The AFT works to stop the loss of productive farmland and to promote farming practices that lead to a healthy environment. Its action-oriented programs include public education, technical assistance in policy development, and direct farmland protection projects. To find out more about the specific steps your community can take to create a farm plan, call the American Farmland Trust at 202-331-7300 or visit http://www.farmland.org.

Resources for Living Local

Why Save Farms?

- *Farms feed America.*

- *Farms contribute to the scenic open spaces of the nation's countryside.*

- *Farms provide a direct link to national agricultural heritage.*

- *Farmland offers important wildlife habitat and acts as a buffer between urban and wilderness areas.*

- *Farms contribute more in taxes than they require in services, whereas sprawling residential development demands more than it contributes.*

A Farm Woman's Opinion

by Marion Long
Bowlan
Farmer and
member of the
National
Commission on
Small Farms

Most days it's hard for me to imagine there could be any better place on earth to live than our small family farm in the heart of Pennsylvania Dutch country. We farm land that is the most productive nonirrigated land in the United States. The flower gardens surrounding our farmstead stand as living memorials to three generations of women who share a passion for growing and a love of the land.

To me, being a family farmer is important for reasons beyond financial gain. The lasting values I have learned by living and working on a farm—and that I hope to pass on to my children—are my reasons for persevering. Besides parenting, no other occupation is so grounded in humility. Battling the forces of Mother Nature teaches respect and genuine stewardship. Good husbandry promotes nurturing and caring. Working as a family unit imparts responsibility and a feeling of self-worth. The strength, self-reliance, hardiness, and resilience we gain as a family can never be taken away, even if the farm is.

Family-owned farms offer diversity of ownership, landscape, culture, tradition, and cropping systems. Farmers make meaningful financial and social contributions to their local schools, churches, businesses, and communities. It is better for our rural communities to have 60 farmers with 60 cows than it is to have one farmer with 3,600 cows.

Even so, the national loss of 30,000 family farms every year in favor of industrialized corporate agriculture is unrelenting. In a single generation, 95 percent of African-American farmers in the United States have disappeared. The farmer's share of the food dollar has dropped to an all-time low, and farmers are twice as likely to live in poverty as are members of the general population.

We lament the loss of family farms, but what are we doing to change failing agricultural policies? Our current policies and programs favor large farms over small farms. The continuing consolidation and industrialization of agriculture destroy both market competition and, with that, the opportunity for farmers to earn a fair price for their products.

We can and need to act now. We can make policy choices that provide greater economic opportunity in farming. Three-quarters of U.S. farmland is still owned by family farmers like me. In January 1998, U.S. Department of Agriculture (USDA) secretary Dan Glickman received from the USDA National Commission on Small Farms a comprehensive set of policy recommendations entitled A Time to Act.* The recommendations outline a national policy to benefit family-size farms . The commission recommended policy shifts that would encourage the use of low-cost production methods, spur the growth of farmer-owned cooperatives, develop direct markets to consumers, enforce antitrust laws, and provide the tools and incentives for the next generation to enter agriculture.

If the USDA and Congress have the courage to act on those recommendations, our children could enjoy the legacy of an enduring farm community. I want my children to have that opportunity; certainly, others want the same. We can fix this problem if we have the will and the spirit to do so.

*For information on how to help in the implementation of the National Commission on Small Farms' recommendations, contact the Center for Rural Affairs, P.O. Box 406, Walthill, NE 68067, 402-846-5428.

Possibly the most important question we can ask our produce manager is, "Where do these apples come from?" or "Where did you get those berries?" Shoppers should be encouraged to choose locally grown produce and encourage stores to stock products from regional farmers. That means being aware of what's fresh in your region according to season. Discerning customers will not unquestioningly accept a supermarket's "local" designation for fruit that they know is not grown in their area. And if you have any doubt, you should speak up.

Getting Locally Grown Foods into Supermarkets

Buying locally grown food isn't always convenient. Although farmers markets and community-supported agriculture farms are increasing in numbers, most food is still purchased at grocery stores. Large grocery stores are often set up to buy from existing distribution systems rather than directly from farmers. But grocers are eager to meet customer needs and will be more willing to carry local if they feel that there is sufficient demand. If your supermarket carries few or no local farm products there are several steps that you can take to encourage it to do so.

1. Begin by gathering signatures on a petition asking the store manager to stock regionally grown foods. Point out that you are regular customers and that you are concerned about the foods you feed your family. Once you have gathered at least 30 signatures, submit the petition to the store manager or to the regional manager. Be sure to keep a copy of the petition for your own records.

2. Encourage your friends and neighbors to write letters to the store or to talk to the produce manager when they are in the store. Success is more likely if the supermarket management sees that there is a consistent public demand in your community for locally grown foods.

3. Make a call to your supermarket within a week after mailing the petition to set up a meeting with the supermarket manager and the produce buyer. Organize a small group to attend the meeting with you. Prepare for the meeting, and attend it armed with talking points. These points should include your objectives, the issues you want to raise, and responses to issues that the supermarket representatives are likely to raise.

Your objectives: You are asking the supermarket management to make more locally grown produce available in the store, to provide attractive displays and point-of-purchase information about how and where this produce is grown, and to actively encourage the store's suppliers to use practices that reduce or eliminate reliance on pesticides and other hazardous agricultural products.

Mothers & Others for a Livable Planet adapted from the Green Food Shopper

Your concerns: Be sure to let the store manager know if shoppers in your group are now seeking out locally grown foods elsewhere. State your reasons for wanting locally grown foods: freshness, less likelihood that it has been treated with postharvest chemicals, and support for family farmers and the local economy. Emphasize your reasons for wanting local foods that are grown with few or no pesticides: concern about the health and environmental problems surrounding pesticide use, children's susceptibility to some of the toxic effects of pesticides, and the desire to support growers who take responsibility for protecting the local environment and the health of their workers and neighbors.

Their concerns: Stores often use the argument that shoppers won't buy imperfect-looking produce. The quality of organic food has greatly improved, so that in many cases, organic produce looks as good as conventional. When organic produce has cosmetic imperfections, the latter are usually insignificant. Studies show that when customers are given point-of-purchase information—such as attractive signs explaining how and why food was grown without pesticides—they prefer produce grown without pesticides even if it is imperfect looking. Price is the other thing often cited by store managers. Organic can cost more because more intensive management went into producing it, and local produce can carry the added cost of high land and labor expenses that comes from locating near major cities. Careful and creative purchasing can help keep prices in line.

4. Get the word out through your local media. You can write letters to the editor about the need for better food choices or provide a small newspaper with an editorial on the issue.

5. Whether or not the store management seems interested in responding to your request, have a follow-up meeting with them 4 to 6 weeks later. Be sure to set up this follow-up meeting during your first meeting. This follow-up meeting should focus on the store's progress and plans to date. Continue to monitor the store's progress, and be sure to acknowledge any progress that you see.

Finally, remember that there are two sides to this deal. In your meetings and correspondence, assure the store that you will support it with your purchases if it commits to your goals. Let the management know that you will spread the word to its customers about the changes the store is making. And use your food dollars to support the stores that commit to providing a market for local farm products.

Alice Waters, the doyenne of the create-your-menu-straight-from-the-garden movement, says simply, "They get it once they eat it." What they get is the intense flavor that comes from ingredients picked fresh and grown in a caring and respectful manner. Like Waters, chefs, farmers, food enthusiasts, environmentalists, and educators across the country are making the flavorful connection between what we eat and how—and even where—that food is grown.

While many people believe that eating from the farm—particularly the organic farm—offers the healthiest diet, the best reasons to go local, seasonal, and organic are freshness and flavor. In homes bursting with cutting-edge cookware and high-tech kitchen gadgets, there is not a single mechanical contrivance that can replicate the flavor of a peach grown in living, chemical-free soil and eaten within 48 hours of being picked. That's why chefs are turning to local farms for ingredients and why home cooks are shopping at farmers markets or joining community-supported-agriculture (CSA) farms.

How often do you walk through your produce section noticing where the pears were grown? or the avocados? or the peppers? Try it. You may be surprised to learn how much of what you're eating is grown thousands of miles away. Small, independent farmers are put at risk when they are forced to compete in a global market. While California produces a wide array of fresh produce year-round, it should not be taken for granted that your local farms are going to be there next year.

For years, rich, productive farmland in this country has been destroyed to make way for new construction while farming dissolved into a centralized, factorylike endeavor. In the world of corporate farming, there is little incentive to grow any of the countless varieties of heirloom tomatoes in existence or to choose flavor over so-called cost-efficiency. Only small family farms—the ones that benefit from and contribute to your community—are going to work to keep the soil alive, to grow the most flavorful produce, and to raise the best-tasting farm animals in the most humane way possible. Read how the farmers in this book care for the land they farm. Is there any question in your mind that theirs is the food you want on your table?

Finally, food is about being nourished, both physically and spiritually. It's about sitting around a table with loved ones at holidays and mealtimes. It's about the pleasure we feel hunting for the best ingredients. We remember the places our parents and grandparents shopped because no one else had it fresher. They knew the farmers, the purveyors, the butchers, and the shopkeepers. The products they bought were more than just brands; there were real people behind those brands, and often those people were friends and neighbors.

Farms add beauty to the landscape, provide jobs in their communities, and create educational opportunities for children. And when you live near a small family farm, you're steps away from fresh, delicious produce. Choose to keep your local farms part of your community.

Eat Fresh, Eat Local

by Wendy Rickard
Eating Fresh Publications

SEASONAL AVAILABILITY*

SEASONAL AVAILABILITY*	JAN	FEB	MAR	APR	MAY	JUN	JUL	AUG	SEP	OCT	NOV	DEC
APPLES								X	X	X	X	X
APRICOTS					X	X	X					
ARTICHOKES			X	X	X				X	X	X	
ASPARAGUS			X	X	X							
BASIL					X	X	X	X	X	X		
BEETS	X	X	X	X	X	X	X	X	X	X	X	X
BOK CHOI & TAT SOI	X	X	X	X	X	X	X	X	X	X	X	X
BROCCOLI	X	X	X	X	X	X	X	X	X	X	X	X
CABBAGE—NAPA & SAVOY	X	X	X	X	X	X	X	X	X	X	X	X
CARROTS	X	X	X	X	X	X	X	X	X	X	X	X
CHERRIES					X	X	X					
CORN, SWEET							X	X	X	X		
CUCUMBERS					X	X	X	X	X	X		
EGGPLANT								X	X	X		
ESCAROLE & RADICCHIO	X	X	X	X	X	X	X	X	X	X	X	X
FENNEL	X	X	X	X	X	X	X	X	X	X	X	X
FIGS						X	X	X	X	X		
GREENS—Kale, Collards, Chard, Arugula, Mizuna & Mustard	X	X	X	X	X	X	X	X	X	X	X	X
GRAPES							X	X	X	X		
KIWIS	X	X	X	X						X	X	X
LEEKS	X	X	X	X	X	X	X	X	X	X	X	X
LETTUCE & SALAD MIX	X	X	X	X	X	X	X	X	X	X	X	X
MELONS						X	X	X	X			
ONIONS & GARLIC	X	X		X	X	X	X	X	X	X	X	X
ORANGES & LEMONS	X	X	X	X	X	X						X
PEACHES & NECTARINES						X	X	X	X			
PEARS & ASIAN PEARS							X	X	X	X	X	X
PEPPERS, SWEET & HOT								X	X	X		
PERSIMMONS										X	X	X
POTATOES	X	X	X		X	X	X	X	X	X	X	X
RADISHES	X	X	X	X	X	X	X	X	X	X	X	X
RUTABAGAS & TURNIPS	X	X	X	X	X	X	X	X	X	X	X	X
SCALLIONS	X	X	X	X	X	X	X	X	X	X	X	X
SQUASH, SUMMER					X	X	X	X	X	X		
SQUASH, WINTER	X	X								X	X	X
STRAWBERRIES				X	X	X	X	X	X	X	X	
SWEET POTATOES	X								X	X	X	X
TOMATOES							X	X	X	X		

*SEE PAGE 175 FOR OTHER RESOURCES ON SEASONAL AVAILABILITY

STORAGE/PRESERVATION*	STORAGE	PRESERVATION
APPLES	REFRIGERATE (VP) • ROOT CELLAR: 32°F, MOIST • DRY: 55°F, DARK	SAUCE • APPLE BUTTER • DRY • JUICE • CIDER
APRICOTS	ROOM TEMPERATURE • IF RIPE, REFRIGERATE IN PLASTIC	DRY • FREEZE • JAM • CAN • JUICE
ARTICHOKES	REFRIGERATE (SP) (ADD FEW DROPS WATER)	DRY • FREEZE • CAN • IN OIL
ASPARAGUS	REFRIGERATE (SP)	DRY • FREEZE • CAN
BASIL	REFRIGERATE WITH ROOTS IN WATER	DRY • FREEZE (BLANCHED) • IN OIL • VINEGAR
BEETS	REFRIGERATE (OP) • ROOT CELLAR: 32°F—40°F, MOIST	DRY • FREEZE • CAN • PICKLE
BOK CHOI & TAT SOI	REFRIGERATE (VP) • ROOT CELLAR: 32°F, DAMP	DRY
BROCCOLI	REFRIGERATE (OP) • ROOT CELLAR	FREEZE • DRY • IN OIL
CABBAGE—NAPA, SAVOY	REFRIGERATE (VP)	DRY • FERMENT (SAUERKRAUT)
CARROTS	REFRIGERATE (SP) • ROOT CELLAR: 32°F—40°F, MOIST	DRY • FREEZE • CAN
CHERRIES	REFRIGERATE UNWASHED IN PLASTIC	DRY • FREEZE • CAN • JAM • JUICE
CORN, SWEET	REFRIGERATE IN PLASTIC WITH HUSK ON	DRY • FREEZE • CAN
CUCUMBERS	REFRIGERATE UNWASHED IN PLASTIC AT 45°F—50°F	PICKLE
EGGPLANT	ROOM TEMPERATURE (SHORT TERM), REFRIGERATE IN PLASTIC	DRY • FREEZE AS PART OF PREPARED DISH
ESCAROLE & RADICCHIO	REFRIGERATE (VP) • ROOT CELLAR: 32°F, MOIST	—
FENNEL	REFRIGERATE IN PLASTIC	LEAVES: FREEZE, DRY • SEEDS: DRY
FIGS	REFRIGERATE IN PAPER BAG OR ON PLATE	FREEZE • DRY • CAN
GRAPES	REFRIGERATE (VP) • ROOT CELLAR: 32°F, MOIST	FREEZE • DRY • JUICE • PICKLE • JAM
GREENS—Kale, Collards, Chard, Arugula, Mizuna & Mustard	REMOVE BANDS OR TIES, REFRIGERATE (SP)	FREEZE • DRY • CAN
KIWIS	ROOM TEMPERATURE • IF RIPE, REFRIGERATE	FREEZE IN SYRUP
LEEKS	REMOVE BANDS, REFRIGERATE (OP) • ROOT CELLAR: 32°F, MOIST	FREEZE • DRY
LETTUCE & SALAD MIX	REMOVE BANDS, REFRIGERATE (VP) UNWASHED	FIRM LETTUCE CAN BE USED IN SAUERKRAUT
MELONS	ROOM TEMPERATURE (IF HARD) • REFRIGERATE 40°F—45°F	FREEZE
ONIONS & GARLIC	DRY STORE: COOL, DRY, WELL VENTILATED, DARK (GARLIC)	FREEZE (ONIONS) • DRY • PICKLED • IN OIL
ORANGES & LEMONS	ROOM TEMPERATURE (COOL) • REFRIGERATE (LONGER STORAGE)	DRY • CAN • MARMALADE • JUICE • SALT (LEMONS)
PEACHES & NECTARINES	ROOM TEMPERATURE • IF RIPE, REFRIGERATE	FREEZE • DRY • CAN • JAM • JUICE
PEARS & ASIAN PEARS	ROOM TEMPERATURE • IF RIPE, REFRIGERATE	DRY • CAN • SAUCE • PICKLE • PEAR BUTTER • JUICE
PEPPERS, SWEET & HOT	ROOM TEMPERATURE (COOL) • REFRIGERATE (LONGER STORAGE)	FREEZE • DRY • CAN • PICKLED • SAUCE • IN OIL
PERSIMMONS	ROOM TEMPERATURE • IF RIPE, REFRIGERATE	FREEZE • DRY • JAM
POTATOES	DRY: COOL, DARK, WELL VENTILATED • ROOT CELLAR: 40°F, MOIST	DRY • CAN • FLOUR • STARCH
RADISHES	REMOVE GREENS, REFRIGERATE (OP) • ROOT CELLAR: 32°F, MOIST	PICKLE
RUTABAGAS & TURNIPS	REFRIGERATE IN PLASTIC • ROOT CELLAR: 32°F, MOIST	FREEZE • CAN (FERMENTED)
SCALLIONS	REMOVE BANDS, REFRIGERATE IN PLASTIC	FREEZE OR PICKLE AS PART OF PREPARED DISH
SQUASH, SUMMER	REFRIGERATE IN PLASTIC: 41°F—50°F	FREEZE • DRY • CAN
SQUASH, WINTER	DRY STORE: 50°F—55°F, DARK, WELL VENTILATED	FREEZE • CAN
STRAWBERRIES	ROOM TEMPERATURE (EAT THAT DAY) • REFRIGERATE: DRY, AIRTIGHT	FREEZE • DRY • JAM
SWEET POTATOES	DRY STORE: 55°F—60°F, DARK, WELL VENTILATED	FREEZE • DRY • CAN
TOMATOES	ROOM TEMPERATURE (62°F—68°F), HUMID, OUT OF DIRECT SUN	DRY • CAN • IN OIL • IN SALT • JUICE • JELLY • SAUCE

*SEE PAGE 175 FOR OTHER RESOURCES ON STORAGE & PRESERVATION
JAM IS USED TO INDICATE SOME FORM OF FRUIT PRESERVE: JAM, JELLY, PRESERVE, OR CONSERVE.
VP = VENTED PLASTIC BAG • SP = SEALED PLASTIC BAG • OP = OPEN PLASTIC BAG

When You Can't Buy Local,
Buy Organic: It's an International Statement

by Carl Smith
Senior editor
Foundation for
Advancements in
Science and
Education

Consumers thinking of switching to organic produce typically consider doing so for matters of health. In a world of smog, uncertain drinking water, and nonstop industrial chemical emission, the grocery cart seems to be one place where we can draw the line.

Ours, however, is not the only health affected by our food choices. The choices we make in the produce section have international consequences as well. The steady stream of imported, out-of-season fruits and vegetables we have come to expect come at a price, and the possibility of pesticide residues on our broccoli is the least of it.

In tropical areas, pesticides may be applied 25 to 50 times a year or more. A World Resources Institute review of the Latin American export agriculture boom says that "the very high inputs of pesticides commonly used in most NTAEs (nontraditional agricultural exports) have impaired workers' health, posed risks to consumers from residues in food," and "brought on pesticide resistance and environmental disruptions."[1]

Even though only 20 percent of agricultural use occurs in developing countries, those areas account for more than 99 percent of all deaths from pesticide poisoning, according to estimates published in the *British Journal of Industrial Medicine*.[2] The World Health Organization's *World Health Statistics Quarterly* has reported that as many as 25 million agricultural workers in the developing world may suffer at least one incident of pesticide poisoning each year, because they do not use the U.S.-required protective clothing or respirators or because they receive no training.[3]

Other things can make workers susceptible to poisoning. Protein deficiency and water deprivation—common among the rural poor in developing countries—can increase the toxic effect of pesticides. Many pesticides accumulate in human fat tissue. Because such fat stores are used for nourishment by the body, the pesticide residues stored in fat may be released into the bloodstream, thereby creating new exposures.[4] Migrant laborers in developing countries live in conditions of constant exposure to pesticide residues on their food, clothing, and household furnishings and in the water available for drinking and bathing.[5] Exposure away from the fields is not limited to migrant workers; farmers in developing countries commonly store pesticides in their homes.[6,7,8]

It should be underscored that this labor force includes millions of children. The International Labour Organization (ILO) reported in 1997 that 90 percent of rural working children in the developing world are engaged in agriculture-related activities.[9] In some countries, nearly a third of the agricultural workforce is composed of children. Rural children, girls in particular, begin their economic activity as young as 5, 6, or 7 years of age. According to the ILO, children can be found "mixing, loading and applying pesticides, fertilizers and herbicides."[10] The ILO says that "exposure to pesticides, notably in agricultural sectors, is a major cause of infant mortality."[11]

UNICEF echoes that unsettling picture: "Children pick crops still dripping with pesticides or spray the chemicals themselves. . . eight- to 10-hour days are not uncommon—and spent far from running water," states the 1997 edition of *State of the World's Children*.[12]

All of this might seem a bit overwhelming to a shopper who isn't looking much beyond dinner. On the other hand, it could be viewed as an opportunity for public service. Interest in reducing chemical inputs is growing in developing countries for both economic and environmental reasons. Those efforts will flourish to the extent that if choosing imported produce, consumers, retailers, and chefs purchase organic produce coming from those regions.

So consider adding this spice to your cabinet: the knowledge that the decision to use organic ingredients is a contribution toward better lives for others halfway across the globe. Multiplied over and over again, such a decision could have a profound impact on millions.

References

1 L. A. Thrupp. Bittersweet Harvest for Global Supermarkets: Challenges in Latin America's Agricultural Export Boom. Washington, D.C.: World Resources Institute, 1995.

2 J. Jeyaratnam. "Health Problems of Pesticide Usage in the Third World." *British Journal of Industrial Medicine* 42:505–506, 1985.

3 J. Jeyaratnam. "Acute Pesticide Poisoning: A Major Global Health Problem." *World Health Statistics Quarterly* 43(3): 139–144, 1990.

4 Public Health Impact of Pesticides Used in Agriculture: Report of a WHO/UNEP working group. Geneva: World Health Organization, 1989.

5 A. Wright. The Death of Ramón González. Austin, Texas: University of Texas Press, 1990.

6 C. C. Crissman, D. C. Cole, F. Carpio. "Pesticide Use and Farm Worker Health in Ecuadorian Potato Production." *American Journal of Agricultural Economics* 76:593–597, 1994.

7 L. A. Thrupp. "Exporting Risk Analyses to Developing Countries." *Global Pesticide Campaigner*. 4(1):3–5, 1994.

8 L. Castillo, C. Wesseling. "Pesticide Problems in Central America: A Regional Approach." *Global Pesticide Campaigner* 4(2): 3–5, 1992.

9 International Labour Organization: "Amsterdam Conference Boosts Campaign against Child Labour." *World of Work* 20, 1997.

10 International Labour Organization: "Child Labour: Targeting the Intolerable." Geneva: ILO, 1996.

11 ILO, op cit.

12 C. Bellamy. *The State of the World's Children,* 1997. London: Oxford University Press, 1997.

The United States routinely exports to developing countries certain pesticides that are either banned or unsafe under the existing conditions of use. According to U.S. Customs documents, in 1995 and 1996 at least 21 million pounds of pesticides that are forbidden for use in the United States were exported from U.S. ports—an average rate of more than 14 tons per day. During that same period, pesticides the World Health Organization has designated as "extremely hazardous" were exported at an average rate of 1.4 tons per hour.

Resources for Living Local

Californians For Pesticide Reform
is a coalition of more than 120 public health, consumer, environmental, sustainable agriculture, labor, and rural assistance public interest organizations that work to expand the public's right to know about pesticide use and abuse. It also works to reduce that use and promote safer, ecologically sound agriculture and urban pest management.

The Natural Step to Sustainability

Do you ever feel overwhelmed by what we're doing to the earth and wonder whether we really can create a sustainable future? Can you imagine a land in which:

- Farmers saved money and the environment by reducing overall pesticide use by 75 percent in less than one decade
    - Hundreds of thousands of young people became concerned about the earth and created their own environmental projects, computer networks, video programs, and a youth parliament
    - More than 70 cities became ecomunicipalities, thereby decreasing costs and waste while creating more jobs
- Sixty major corporations cleaned up their act and began offering ecologically sound products and services that increased profitability, reduced pollution, and provided competitive advantage
- The largest oil company developed clean, farmer-grown biofuels and lobbied the government to raise air-quality standards
- Even McDonald's served veggie burgers and organic milk while making a commitment to go completely organic
- All of this was supported by the king and queen through annual environmental awards

Would you like to live in a land like that? You can. Sweden has already accomplished it and more. And the ideas behind Swenden's success are spreading around the world—in part through an initiative called the Natural Step (TNS), a consensus framework for understanding and addressing environmental problems.

Journey of the Natural Step

Launched in 1989 as a nonprofit educational organization, TNS was the brainchild of Swedish physician and cancer researcher Karl-Henrik Robert. Concerned about rising cancer rates among children, Robert's research convinced him the causes were connected to environmental factors, not lifestyle. He began a consensus-building process among his fellow researchers on the conditions for planetary sustainability. After 21 drafts of a paper, Robert achieved consensus from 50 leading Swedish scientists. But he knew that to bring about real change, he needed to creatively engage people and reach out to the broader public.

Robert persuaded major corporations that they should support an effort to send an audiocassette and an educational pamphlet on the findings to every home and school in Sweden, 4.3 million altogether. Since then, there has been an impressive series of shifts. More than 60

by Terry Gips
President
Sustainability
Associates

corporations in Sweden have implemented TNS, including the world's largest manufacturers of appliances (Electrolux) and furniture (Ikea), Swedish Railways, three major supermarket chains (ICA, Konsum, and Hemkop), the largest hotel chain (Scandic), and even McDonald's.

The Core of the Natural Step

TNS was established with the purpose of developing and sharing a common framework composed of easily understood, scientifically based principles that serve as a compass to guide society toward a just and sustainable future. The Natural Step emphasizes that the only long-term, sustainable manner in which business and society can operate is within the earth's natural cycles. This can be accomplished by meeting four basic sustainability conditions (see next page). It is being shared successfully through one-day seminars with businesses, nonprofits, communities, government agencies, schools, and other organizations in the United States.

(continued next page)

Agriculture Takes the Natural Step

For years, a pitched battle raged between Sweden's organic and conventional farmers. The Natural Step (TNS) sought to bring the two groups together by using a modification of its original consensus process. After an often challenging two-year process, both sides agreed on a forward-thinking TNS Agricultural Consensus document. The Farmers Union declared a new goal: On our way to the cleanest agriculture in the world. Incorporating TNS ideas, the Farmers Union transformed its Sanga-Saby Conference Center into the world's most environmentally conscious conference facility while also becoming profitable. The union also turned both its model farm and its restaurant completely organic, and it's gone fossil-fuel-free, with vehicles run on clean-burning, farmer-grown canola fuel.

To top this off, Swedish farmers achieved a 75 percent reduction in pesticide use within a decade. First, they met a national 50-percent-pesticide-use-reduction goal, which they achieved in five years. Then they initiated a further 50 percent reduction goal, which they achieved in only four years. This benefited both the environment and farmers' bottom lines.

Using a similar approach, TNS founder Karl-Henrik Robert and TNS have developed consensus processes and papers on other thorny topics such as energy, forestry, mining, and municipalities. TNS is currently engaged in its first open, international consensus process to address the challenging issue of genetic engineering.

A Sustainable Future?

The Natural Step's vision of creating a sustainable planet within our lifetimes may seem outlandish, but we shouldn't forget that President John Kennedy once put forth the bold dream of landing a human being on the moon. Many scoffed at the idea, but Kennedy was able to inspire a nation to unite behind that shared vision. And the nation succeeded.

Now it's time for us to return home to fulfill the dream of a sustainable future for the earth. The Natural Step can be a useful tool in guiding us on our journey. We can save money and the earth while meeting basic human needs. Together we can make our dreams a reality.

TNS Four Conditions for Sustainability

1. Reduce Mining and Use of Fossil Fuels
Substances from the earth's crust must not systematically increase in nature. This means that fossil fuels, metals, and other minerals must not be extracted at a faster rate than their slow redeposit into the earth's crust. There are great opportunities for shifting to renewable energy from the burning of coal and petroleum, which are creating dangerous levels of invisible pollutants and global climatic change. We can reduce the use of chemical fertilizers and expand the reuse and recycling of metals in order to reduce the spread of hazards from mining, processing, and use of metals.

2. Eliminate Persistent Human-Made Toxins
Substances produced by society must not systematically increase in nature. This means that substances must not be produced faster than they can be broken down and reintegrated into the cycles of nature. We can support organic agriculture and eliminate the use of DDT, PCBs, and other hazardous chemicals while stopping factory farm feedlots from causing water and air pollution.

3. Protect Biodiversity and Ecosystems
The physical basis for the productivity and diversity of nature must not be systematically deteriorated. This means the productive surfaces of nature must not be diminished in quality or quantity, and we must not harvest more from nature than can be re-created and renewed. We can safeguard endangered species and ensure sustainable use of our farmland, forests, and waters.

4. Efficiently Meet Human Needs
There must be just and efficient use of resources with respect to meeting human needs. This means that basic human needs must be met with the most resource-efficient methods possible, including equitable resource distribution. We can meet basic human needs through more efficient design that will save money and resources.

CREAMER POTATO & CARAMELIZED ONION PIZZA
WITH FONTINA CHEESE & FRESH ARUGULA
    Anne Gingrass, Hawthorne Lane 144

BUTTERNUT SQUASH BISQUE
    Gary Danko, Gary Danko 146

MEDALLIONS OF LAMB WITH SUN-DRIED CRANBERRIES & PINOT NOIR
    Dan Berman, Mixx 147

LAMB MEAT LOAF WITH GARLIC BUTTERMILK MASHED POTATOES & SAUTEED CHANTERELLES
    Ralph Tingle, Bistro Ralph 148

PUMPKIN CHEESECAKE WITH A CHOCOLATE HAZELNUT CRUST
    Thomas Vinolus, Bittersweet Bistro 150

SEARED RARE AHI SUSPENDED IN LEMON/BLACK PEPPER GELÉE
    Daniel Patterson, Elisabeth Daniel 152

WARM FLAN OF LAURA CHENEL GOAT CHEESE WITH BELL PEPPER PUREE
    Michael Quigley, Cafe Lolo 153

PETITE AÏOLI: AHI TUNA, POTATO & VEGETABLE SALAD
    David Kinch, Restaurant Sent Sovi 154

APPLE TARTE TATIN WITH CIDER SAUCE
    Nancy Oakes, Boulevard 155

ROASTED WHOLE SEA BASS WITH POTATOES & PORCINI
    Reed Hearon, Rose Pistola 156

A STEW OF ARTICHOKES, BUTTERNUT SQUASH & CLAMS
IN A LEMON, GARLIC, SAFFRON, OREGANO SAUCE
    Jesse Cool, Flea Street Café 158

FARFALLE PASTA WITH ROASTED PUMPKIN & A PUMPKIN SEED–ANCHO CHILI PESTO
    Eric Tucker, Millennium 159

SALT & PEPPER SPARERIBS WITH ROASTED APPLESAUCE
    Judy Rodgers, Zuni 160

FRITTO MISTO OF ARTICHOKES, FENNEL & LEMON
    Jody Denton, Restaurant LuLu 161

ROASTED GYPSY PEPPER, RONDE DE NICE SQUASH & TOSCANO CHEESE BREAD PUDDING
    Frances Wilson, Lalime's 162

SMOKED GOAT CHEDDAR & WHITE CORN CHOWDER
    Frances Wilson, Lalime's 163

ROASTED POTATOES & RED ONIONS
    Paul Bertolli, Oliveto 164

CROSTINI WITH WARM CANNELLINI BEANS & WILTED GREEN GULCH CHARD
    Annie Somerville, Greens 165

BAKED APPLE WITH CREAM CHEESE, WALNUTS & CURRANTS WITH APPLE CIDER CREAM
    Bradley Ogden, Lark Creek Inn 166

BUTTERNUT SQUASH, CABBAGE & PANCETTA RISOTTO WITH BASIL OIL
    George Cronk, Park Grill 168

TWICE-BAKED PARMESAN SOUFFLÉ WITH ROMANO BEANS & FRENCH BUTTER PEARS
    Wendy Brucker, Rivoli 169

*Fall
Recipes*

Creamer Potato & Caramelized Onion Pizza
with Fontina Cheese & Fresh Arugula

YIELDS 3 EIGHT-INCH PIZZAS

For the dough:

1 pound bread flour (baker's flour), or 3¹/₂ cups plus 1 tablespoon

1 cup warm water

1 tablespoon honey

¹/₄ ounce fresh yeast or ¹/₄ package dry

2 teaspoons salt

1 tablespoon virgin olive oil

For the pizzas:

6 creamer potatoes or any small, waxy type of potato about 1 inch in diameter

3 cipollini onions or any small, sweet onion about 1 inch in diameter, peeled

1 tablespoon plus 1 teaspoon extra virgin olive oil

1 teaspoon sugar

¹/₄ cup balsamic vinegar

9 to 12 ounces grated Fontina cheese (Swedish if you can find it)

1 tablespoon fresh thyme, chopped

2 to 3 ounces Parmesan cheese, grated

3 small bunches of arugula, washed, stems removed, and torn into large pieces

1. To prepare the dough, combine the flour, water, honey, yeast, salt, and olive oil in a large mixing bowl and mix to make a uniform ball.

2. Place the dough on a lightly floured work surface and knead by hand for 5 or 6 minutes or until the dough becomes smooth and elastic. Cover with a damp towel and allow to rest for 30 minutes in a warm place: 70° to 90°F.

Hawthorne Lane
San Francisco
Anne Gingrass
Executive Chef/
Proprietor

3. Flatten the dough slightly and divide into 6 equal pieces of about 4¹/₂ ounces each. Roll 3 pieces of dough into smooth balls, stretching the dough as tightly as possible. Cover the dough with a damp cloth and let it rest for 30 minutes. Freeze the extra dough to use at another time.

4. To prepare the vegetables, place the potatoes in cold water and bring to a boil. Cook until a sharp paring knife slides easily into the center — about 7 minutes. Remove from the water and cool. Then peel and slice into ¹/₄-inch slices. Sauté the onions in 1 tablespoon of the olive oil until browned on both sides. Add sugar and balsamic vinegar to the pan, reduce the heat, and simmer until the onions become soft. Cool and separate into rings.

5. Preheat the oven to 500°F.

6. For each pizza, press a rounded ball of dough from the center toward the outside to make it flat and thin — about 8 to 10 inches in diameter. Leave about a ¹/₂-inch lip around the edge. Top with the grated Fontina cheese followed by the sliced potatoes, onion rings, thyme, and grated Parmesan. Bake on a pizza stone or a lightly oiled pizza pan for about 10 minutes or until the edges of the crust become golden brown and the cheese melts and begins to bubble.

7. Toss the arugula leaves in 1 teaspoon of the virgin olive oil and sprinkle over the pizzas to garnish.

Chef's Recommendation: Chianti

Butternut Squash Bisque

SERVES 8

4 tablespoons butter

1 large onion, peeled and diced

2 butternut squash, peeled and diced

2 golden delicious apples, peeled, cored, and diced

2 quarts chicken stock or water

1 bay leaf

1 sprig thyme

2 tablespoons honey

2 teaspoons salt or to taste

½ teaspoon pepper

½ cup grated cheddar, Asiago, or Fontina cheese (optional)

2 cups heavy cream (optional)

1. Melt the butter in a large pot. Add the onions and sauté until translucent; this sweetens the onion. Add the squash and apple and sauté for a few more minutes. Cover with the stock and add bay leaf, thyme, and honey. Salt lightly, bring to a boil, and simmer until squash is very soft.

2. Remove bay leaf and thyme. Puree the soup in a food processor or run it through a food mill.

3. Return the soup to the pot. Add pepper and, if desired, the cheese and heavy cream. Stir over a low flame until the cheese is melted and the soup is warm. Serve.

Chef's Recommendation: Gewürztraminer, Joseph Phelps, Napa 1998

GARY DANKO

Gary Danko
San Francisco
Gary Danko
Chef/Owner

Medallions of Lamb
with Sun-Dried Cranberries & Pinot Noir

SERVES 6

12 medallions of lamb, 2 to 3 ounces each

3 tablespoons cracked black peppercorns

Kosher (coarse) salt

2 to 3 tablespoons peanut or corn oil

3 tablespoons shallots, finely minced

⅓ cup sun-dried cranberries, soaked in Pinot Noir to soften

1 cup Pinot Noir

1 cup rich chicken stock

6 tablespoons unsalted butter

2 tablespoons Italian parsley, coarsely chopped

Matchstick Sweet Potatoes (see sidebar)

1. Pat lamb medallions dry with paper towels. Coat evenly with pepper and a good pinch of salt. Lightly pound medallions with meat pounder or cover with waxed paper and press firmly with the heel of your hand to embed crust of pepper and salt.

2. Set skillet over high heat and lightly coat with oil. When oil begins to smoke, add steaks, a few at a time so you do not crowd the pan. Sear for 2 to 3 minutes on each side until brown and crusty. Meat should be rare. Remove from pan and keep warm. Add more oil to pan, if necessary, and repeat until all the medallions are cooked.

3. For sauce, pour excess oil from the skillet. Put skillet back on heat. Add shallots and sauté, stirring with a wooden spoon to bring up drippings, but do not brown. You need to be careful because the pan is hot. Add cranberries. Heat and stir to lightly plump. Add wine and reduce by one-third. Add chicken stock and reduce by half, until sauce just begins to thicken. Add any juices from lamb and whisk in butter.

4. Place lamb back in the pan, basting for about 1 minute to reheat meat to medium rare. Divide meat evenly onto plates, 2 medallions each. Season sauce with salt and pepper to taste, and add parsley. Lightly ladle sauce on meat. Garnish with Matchstick Sweet Potatoes.

Chef's Recommendation: Pinot Noir, Williams Selyem, Hirsch Vineyards, Sonoma Coast 1996

Matchstick Sweet Potatoes

2 large, evenly sized sweet potatoes or yams

2 to 3 tablespoons light olive oil

Salt to taste

Preheat oven to 450°F.

Peel sweet potatoes; cutting potatoes lengthwise, slice into matchsticks, ¼-inch thick, dropping sticks into cold water to retard darkening.

Dry thoroughly with paper towels, and in a small bowl, toss potatoes, olive oil, and salt until matchsticks are thoroughly coated.

Place in a single layer on a cookie sheet, and roast until soft, about 15 to 20 minutes.

Mixx
Santa Rosa
Dan Berman
Chef/Proprietor

Lamb Meat Loaf
with Garlic Buttermilk Mashed Potatoes
& Sautéed Chanterelles

SERVES 6

2 cups unseasoned croutons

1 cup chicken stock

3½ pounds lean ground lamb

2 tablespoons chopped fresh thyme

2 tablespoons chopped fresh parsley

1 teaspoon chopped fresh rosemary

⅓ cup tomato paste

1 small onion, finely chopped

2 whole eggs

Salt and freshly ground black pepper

5 tablespoons minced fresh garlic

4 slices smoked bacon

6 large russet potatoes, peeled and cut in half

Virgin olive oil

1 cup buttermilk

4 tablespoons unsalted butter, at room temperature

2 teaspoons freshly ground white pepper

Sautéed Chanterelles (see sidebar on next page)

1. Soak the croutons in the chicken stock, stirring occasionally, until all the stock is absorbed, about 1 hour.

2. While the croutons are soaking, in a large bowl combine the ground lamb with the thyme, parsley, rosemary, tomato paste, onion, eggs, salt, pepper, and 2 tablespoons of the garlic. Mix well. When the croutons have absorbed all the chicken stock, add them to the lamb mixture.

Bistro Ralph
Healdsburg
Ralph Tingle
Chef/Owner

3. In a baking dish, form the lamb mixture into a loaf approximately 4 inches wide and 1 foot long. Arrange the bacon on top of the meat loaf, along its length, side by side. Cover the meat loaf and bacon loosely with wax paper and let rest in the refrigerator for 1 hour before cooking.

4. Preheat oven to 350°F. Bake the meat loaf for 45 minutes or until it reaches an internal temperature of 145°F on an instant-read thermometer.

5. Start boiling the potatoes at the same time as—or just before—the meat loaf goes into the oven. In a medium-size saucepan, cover the potatoes with cold water, bring to a boil, and simmer for 40 minutes or until a fork easily pierces the potatoes. Strain well. Wipe the inside of the pot dry with a paper towel and return the potatoes to the pot. Place over medium heat and, taking care not to scorch them, stir the potatoes about a minute to dry them. They should become white and fluffy on the outside edges.

6. Sauté the remaining 3 tablespoons of garlic in a small amount of olive oil until soft. Add the sautéed garlic, buttermilk, and butter to the potatoes. Season with salt and the white pepper. Using a large, stiff whisk, whip until fluffy. Show them who's boss! Adjust consistency with buttermilk.

7. Serve the meat loaf, mashed potatoes, and sauteed chanterelles immediately, or hold in a warm oven for a short while.

Chef's Recommendation: Zinfandel

Sautéed Chanterelles

2 pounds chanterelles

4 tablespoons virgin olive oil

1 tablespoon minced garlic

2 tablespoons chopped parsley

Salt and freshly ground black pepper

2 tablespoons brandy

Split the chanterelles by hand, and then sauté in olive oil with garlic, parsley, salt, pepper, and a splash of brandy.

**Local Foods
Local Flavors**

SCIABICA'S

Nick Sciabica & Sons began pressing olive oil in California in 1936 with techniques that Nicola (Nick) Sciabica had learned in Sicily at the turn of the previous century. Joseph, his son, who founded the company with Nicola, continues to produce California olive oils—with his two sons Nicholas and Daniel—using completely natural methods and taking only the first pressing from the olive. The Sciabica family specializes in producing 100 percent varietal cold pressed extra virgin olive oils from as many as eight different varieties of California olives.

Pumpkin Cheesecake
with a Chocolate Hazelnut Crust

SERVES 10 TO 12

For the crust:

1³/₄ cup finely ground chocolate wafers

¹/₄ cup toasted and finely ground hazelnuts

¹/₄ cup brown sugar

4 tablespoons sweet butter, melted

For the filling:

1 pound cream cheese, room temperature

1 cup sugar

¹/₂ vanilla bean, split lengthwise and scraped to release seeds

1 tablespoon cornstarch

¹/₄ teaspoon salt

1 pinch freshly grated nutmeg

¹/₄ teaspoon freshly ground cinnamon

¹/₄ teaspoon ground ginger

4 eggs, room temperature

4 egg whites, room temperature

¹/₂ cup heavy or whipping cream

2 teaspoons fresh lemon juice

17 ounces mascarpone cheese, room temperature

1 pound fresh pumpkin puree

The day before serving:

1. Preheat oven to 350°F.

2. To prepare the crust, place wafer crumbs, nuts, and sugar in a mixer with a paddle. Add butter and mix until incorporated. Place crumb mixture into a 10-inch buttered and parchment-lined cake pan or into a 10-inch springform pan with a tight seal. Spread the mixture well to

Bittersweet
B I S T R O

Bittersweet Bistro
Aptos
Thomas Vinolus
Chef/Proprietor

cover the bottom of the pan, pressing firmly to compact. Bake for about 10 minutes and let cool.

3. Reduce oven to 325°F.

4. In a mixer with a paddle, beat cream cheese, sugar, vanilla bean seeds, cornstarch, salt, nutmeg, cinnamon, and ginger until smooth. Add the eggs, 1 at a time, beating for 1 minute each and scraping the bowl between additions. Add egg whites, cream, and lemon juice. Mix well, but do not overbeat.

5. By hand, in a separate bowl, mix mascarpone and pumpkin puree until smooth. Combine the mixtures from the two bowls, folding until completely incorporated and smooth. Pour mixture into the prepared crust.

6. Put the cake pan in a large baking dish, place in the lower third of the oven, and pour boiling water into the dish until it reaches about halfway up the cake pan. If you are using a springform pan, first wrap the bottom and sides with aluminum foil to prevent water from seeping in. After 1 hour, check to see if the cake is done. Jiggle the pan. The cheesecake should be uniformly firm with a very slight wiggle in the middle. Be sure to cool fully before refrigerating overnight, loosely covered with plastic wrap.

On the day of serving:

7. About 20 minutes before serving, run a hot knife around the edge of the cake. Place the cake pan in a hot water bath for 1 minute to loosen the crust from the pan. Place a plate covered with plastic wrap over the cake pan, invert cake pan and plate, and tap the pan gently to loosen and release the cake. Place another serving plate on top of the cake and flip it over. For a springform pan, open the spring to remove the side; you can serve the cheesecake right on the pan bottom. Refrigerate for at least 15 minutes. Slice with a hot knife. Enjoy!

Chef's Recommendation: Ferrari-Carano El Dorado Gold Late Harvest 1997

Vegetable Stock

1¹/₂ medium yellow onions, sliced

¹/₂ onion, charred over an open flame

2 carrots, peeled and sliced

¹/₂ head of fennel, sliced

1 leek, sliced

¹/₃ head of celery root, sliced

¹/₃ bunch thyme

Put all ingredients in a nonreactive stockpot. Cover with water. Bring to a boil and simmer for 1 hour. Strain through a fine-mesh sieve.

Note: For the gelée recipe, the stock should be fairly strong. After straining the 1¹/₂ cups needed for the recipe, add more water—enough to cover the vegetables by an inch—and simmer for another hour. Strain and reserve for another use.

restaurant
ELISABETH DANIEL

Elisabeth Daniel
San Francisco
Daniel Patterson
Chef/Owner

Seared Rare Ahi
Suspended in Lemon/Black Pepper Gelée

SERVES 6

Duck fat or olive oil, to coat pan

12 ounces sushi-grade Ahi tuna, cut into strips that when viewed end-on, are triangular and about 1¹/₂ inches per side

Sea salt

1¹/₂ cups Vegetable Stock (see sidebar)

2 packets Knox unflavored gelatin

1¹/₂ teaspoons sea salt

1 cup ice water

¹/₃ cup lemon juice

1 tablespoon cider vinegar

1¹/₂ tablespoons minced chives

Grated zest of 2 lemons

Black pepper

Sel gris for garnish

1. Heat a cast-iron skillet until almost smoking. Add a thin layer of fat to the pan (preferably duck fat, but pure olive oil is fine). Season the tuna generously with salt on all sides, and brown quickly on all sides, leaving the center raw. Remove to a clean plate. Let cool, and slice into ¹/₂-inch pieces.

2. Heat vegetable stock to just below a simmer. Add gelatin and 1 teaspoon of the salt. Whisk to dissolve completely.

3. In a nonreactive mixing bowl, put the ice water, lemon juice, cider vinegar, chives, and lemon zest. Using a pepper mill, grind in about 1 tablespoon black pepper, medium grind. Add the vegetable stock mixture to the bowl and whisk gently to combine. Season to taste with the remaining salt and additional pepper, lemon juice, and cider vinegar.

4. Wrap 6 two-inch cylindrical molds tightly with plastic wrap on one side, or line 6 ramekins with plastic wrap. Put the most attractive tuna slices face down and put a second piece on top. Cover with the gelée mixture, filling each mold to ¹/₂ inch above the tuna. Put into refrigerator until set, about 2 hours.

5. Take plastic off molds, run a thin knife around the inside, and unmold the tuna onto a chilled plate, plastic wrap side up. Garnish with a few grains of sel gris on top and some freshly ground black pepper on the plate around it. *Chef's Recommendation: Blanc de Noirs, Schramsberg 1990*

Warm Flan of Laura Chenel Goat Cheese
with Bell Pepper Puree

SERVES 6

1 pound Laura Chenel goat cheese or other mild, soft goat cheese

1 egg

2 egg yolks

$1/2$ cup heavy cream, reduced to $1/4$ cup (see sidebar)

Salt and freshly ground black pepper to taste

Bell Pepper Puree (see below)

1. Preheat oven to 350°F.

2. Puree the goat cheese, egg, and egg yolks in food processor until smooth. With motor running, slowly add the cooled reduced cream. Stop processor, scrape down the sides of the bowl, and add salt and pepper; process 10 more seconds until mixed thoroughly.

3. Divide mixture into 6 buttered 5-ounce ramekins. Place the ramekins in a baking dish. Create a water bath by adding hot water to dish until it comes halfway up the outside of the ramekins. Cover with aluminum foil (shiny side down) and bake for 40 to 45 minutes. The flan is done when an inserted toothpick comes out clean.

4. Run a hot knife around the edge and invert ramekin onto a plate. Lift off ramekin, and spoon the Bell Pepper Puree around the goat cheese flan. Serve with crusty bread.

Chef's Recommendation: Sauvignon Blanc, Rochioli 1998

Bell Pepper Puree

3 red bell peppers

2 tablespoons extra virgin olive oil

Salt and freshly ground black pepper to taste

Cut peppers in half and remove seeds and thick inner membrane. Fill a large sauté pan with 2 inches of boiling water. Place the peppers in the water, cut side down, and cover tightly. Steam over medium heat until soft, about 15 minutes. Let peppers cool, and puree in blender with the olive oil, salt, and pepper. Strain through a medium strainer, pushing through as many solids as possible. Refrigerate until needed; can be made 1 day ahead.

To reduce cream

Heat 2 to 3 inches of water to boiling in the bottom of a double boiler. Add cream to top, and bring to a simmer—do not let boil. Stir frequently to prevent skin from forming, and watch carefully until cream reaches desired quantity. Let cool, skimming any skin that forms.

Cafe Lolo
Santa Rosa
Michael Quigley
Chef/Owner

**Restaurant
Sent Sovi**
Saratoga
David Kinch
Chef/Owner

Petite Aïoli
Ahi Tuna, Potato & Vegetable Salad

SERVES 4

Juice of 1 lemon

Extra virgin olive oil

Salt and pepper

Aïoli (see sidebar)

1 red pepper, roasted, peeled, and cut into strips

1/2 pound heirloom tomatoes, sliced thin or in wedges

1 pound Ahi tuna, cut into 2-inch cubes

1 pound green beans, blanched and chilled

6 small potatoes, boiled, chilled, and sliced thin

2 large artichokes, trimmed, boiled, and quartered

1 head fennel, blanched or braised and cut into strips

4 eggs, hard-boiled, peeled, and sliced thin

1. Make a simple vinaigrette by whisking together the lemon juice, about 1/3 cup of olive oil, and salt and pepper to taste.

2. Make Aïoli and set aside.

3. Marinate the pepper strips in 1 tablespoon olive oil, salt, and pepper. Season tomatoes with 1/2 tablespoon olive oil and salt. Set aside.

4. Season the tuna cubes with salt and pepper. Heat a medium-size skillet or sauté pan over high heat and sear the tuna on all sides, taking care to leave the center rare or as desired. Set aside.

5. Toss the green beans with the vinaigrette and place a small mound in the center of a serving plate. Arrange the potatoes, tomatoes, artichokes, fennel, egg, and peppers around and on the beans. Slice the tuna as thinly as possible and arrange on the plate.

6. Drizzle with Aïoli at the last moment. Serve at room temperature.

Chef's Recommendation: Vin Gris de Cigare rosé, Bonny Doon, Santa Cruz

Aïoli recipe by Joseph George.

Apple Tarte Tatin
with Cider Sauce

SERVES 8

8 tablespoons butter

1 cup light brown sugar

6 to 8 small, firm, green sour apples or Fuji apples, peeled, cored, and halved

1 sheet of frozen puff pastry

Cider Sauce (see sidebar)

Vanilla ice cream

1. Preheat oven to 425°F.

2. Put the butter and sugar in a heavy, ovenproof 10-inch skillet over medium heat and cook until bubbling. Boil and stir until the mixture turns a deep caramel color, about 5 minutes. Remove the pan from the heat and add the apples, core side up. Return to heat, and, taking care not to let the sauce burn, cook the apples 5 minutes until they begin to caramelize.

3. Cut the puff pastry to match the size of the skillet. Drape the pastry over the apples.

4. Place the skillet in the oven and bake until browned, about 15 to 20 minutes.

5. Remove the skillet from the oven. If the syrup is runny, place the skillet over high heat to thicken. Watch carefully to be sure the syrup doesn't burn or cook completely away. Remove the skillet from the heat and allow it to cool for 10 minutes. Carefully and quickly turn the skillet upside down on a serving dish that has a lip to catch to sauce.* Serve with Cider Sauce and vanilla ice cream.

Chef's Recommendation: Graham's 20-year-old tawny port

*Note: Syrup may spill out as you invert the skillet. Be sure to protect your hands, clothing, and work surface.

Cider Sauce

2 cups apple cider or apple juice

4 tablespoons butter

1/2 cup light brown sugar

Pour the cider or juice into a medium-size saucepan. Boil vigorously over high heat, until it is reduced to 1/2 cup. This will take approximately 15 minutes. Pour the reduced cider/juice into a measuring cup and reserve until ready to use.

In the same saucepan, melt the butter and sugar, shaking pan or stirring to incorporate well. Remove the pan from the heat and add the reduced apple cider or juice. Stir well.

Boulevard
San Francisco
Nancy Oakes
Chef/Owner

Roasted Whole Sea Bass
with Potatoes & Porcini

SERVES 4

4 medium-size potatoes (preferably Yellow Finn), peeled and sliced
  1/2-inch thick

4 cups water

2 teaspoons salt

4 tablespoons olive oil

4 small or 2 medium-size porcini mushrooms (also called cepes), sliced

2 cloves garlic, lightly crushed to release juices

2 teaspoons minced fresh rosemary (1/2 teaspoon dried)

1 two- to three-pound whole sea bass or 4 six-ounce fillets

1 teaspoon black pepper

1. Preheat oven to 425°F.

2. Combine the potatoes, water, and 1 teaspoon of the salt in a small
   saucepan and bring to a simmer. Cook the potatoes for 10 minutes or
   until they are very soft and begin to break apart. Remove the pot from
   the heat and leave the potatoes in their cooking water to cool.

3. Heat 2 tablespoons of the olive oil in a medium-size sauté pan over
   medium-high heat. Add the mushrooms and cook for 5 minutes or until
   they start to brown. Add the garlic and sauté 1 minute. Stir in the
   rosemary and cook 1 minute longer. Add 2 cups of the potato cooking
   water to the mushroom mixture and simmer for about 5 minutes. Add
   the cooked potatoes; remove from the heat. Reserve the remaining
   potato cooking water to use when preparing the sauce.

4. Coat the fish with the remaining 2 tablespoons of olive oil and season
   with black pepper and 1 teaspoon of the salt inside and out. If you are
   using fillets, brush them with oil and sprinkle with salt and pepper.
   Place the fish in a roasting pan or a large ovenproof skillet and pour
   the potato-mushroom mixture into the pan. The liquid should come
   about halfway up the fish.

Rose Pistola

Rose Pistola
San Francisco
Reed Hearon
Chef/Owner

5. Place the fish in the preheated oven. If using whole fish, roast it for approximately 40 minutes or until the flesh is firm to the touch and begins to pull away from the bone easily. If preparing fish fillets, roast the fish for approximately 25 minutes or until the meat is firm to the touch and begins to flake easily.

6. As the fish cooks, the liquid will reduce to a saucelike consistency. If it becomes too thick, add a small amount of the potato water. Serve the liquid as a sauce with the fish.

Chef's Recommendation: Barbera d'Alba, Silvio Grasso 1997

Laura Chenel's Chèvre was founded in 1979. After Laura Chenel apprenticed at four goat cheese–producing farmsteads in France, she expanded her cheese-making hobby into a business. Laura Chenel's Chèvre was the first American company to commercially produce French-style goat cheeses, and its line includes such classics as Taupinière and Fromage Blanc. Laura Chenel's Chèvre has always been committed to producing consistently high-quality, award-winning cheeses.

A Stew of Artichokes, Butternut Squash & Clams
in a Lemon, Garlic, Saffron, Oregano Sauce

SERVES 4

4 large artichokes

2 cups peeled, cubed butternut squash pieces

4 cups chicken or vegetable broth or to just cover

3 tablespoons extra virgin olive oil

1 whole lemon, sliced thin

4 to 6 cloves garlic, peeled and minced

Small pinch of saffron

1 pound fresh clams

2 tablespoons chopped fresh oregano

1 fresh chili pepper, such as cayenne, jalapeño, or habenero, seeded and chopped

$^{1}/_{2}$ teaspoon salt

$^{1}/_{4}$ teaspoon freshly ground pepper

1. Cut off the tips of the artichokes and trim away the outer leaves until the remaining leaves are a lighter yellow-green and look tender. Cut the trimmed artichoke into quarters.

2. Place the artichokes and squash pieces in a large pot and cover them with chicken stock. Add the olive oil, lemon, garlic, and saffron. Cover and simmer over medium heat for 30 minutes or until the artichokes are thoroughly cooked. Take the pot off the heat, remove the artichokes and squash from the pot, and set them aside. Discard the lemon slices and reserve the remaining liquid. Using a spoon, remove the inner thistle or fuzzy choke of the artichoke and discard.

3. Put the pan of liquid back on the stove, bring to a boil, and reduce by half. Add the clams, oregano, and chili peppers. Cover and cook until the clams open. Add back the artichokes and squash, and season with salt and pepper. Serve in shallow bowls—with warm bread for dipping—as a soup or over pasta as an entrée.

Chef's Recommendation: Merlot

Flea Street Café
Menlo Park
Jesse Cool
Chef/Owner

Farfalle Pasta with Roasted Pumpkin
& a Pumpkin Seed–Ancho Chili Pesto

SERVES 4

This well-seasoned, hearty fall pasta dish is compliments of Sous Chef Bruce Enloe. Any firm-fleshed winter squash will work as well as pumpkin. Look for fresh poblano chilies in your local farmers market through October.

³/₄ pound farfalle noodles

1 yellow onion, peeled and sliced into thin crescents

4 tablespoons extra virgin olive oil

1 recipe Roasted Pumpkin (see below)

¹/₄ cup golden raisins, plumped in warm water

2 cups spinach leaves or arugula

Pumpkin Seed–Poblano Chili Pesto (see sidebar)

Salt to taste

2 tablespoons toasted pumpkin seeds, for garnish

1. Cook the farfalle pasta according to package directions. Set aside to cool.

2. In a large sauté pan, sauté the onions in the olive oil over medium heat until the onions are soft and slightly browned. Add the pumpkin, raisins, and spinach and sauté until the spinach is slightly wilted. Add the pesto followed by the pasta. Sauté until heated through. Adjust the salt to taste. Serve garnished with the pumpkin seeds.

Chef's Recommendation: Zinfandel, Sangiovese, Chianti, or beer

Roasted Pumpkin

4 cups peeled, 1-inch-cubed pumpkin or winter squash flesh

1 tablespoon extra virgin olive oil

2 teaspoons ground cumin

½ teaspoon salt

Preheat oven to 400°F. Toss all ingredients together in a bowl. Transfer to a baking pan. Bake 20 minutes, turning the pumpkin after 10 minutes.

Pumpkin Seed–Poblano Chili Pesto

2 poblano chilies, roasted, peeled, and seeded

1½ cups pumpkin seeds, well toasted

4 peeled garlic cloves

½ bunch cilantro, leaves and stems

2 limes, juiced

Salt to taste

1 teaspoon nutritional yeast

2 teaspoons yellow miso (optional)

Water as needed

Blend all ingredients in a food processor. Thin with the water to a spreadable paste. Use or store airtight for up to 4 days.

MILLE☉NNIUM

Millennium
San Francisco
Eric Tucker
Head Chef

ZUNI

Zuni
San Francisco
Judy Rodgers
Chef/Owner

Salt & Pepper Spareribs
with Roasted Applesauce

FOR EACH PERSON:

For the spareribs:
1 pound of pork spareribs, meat and bones, per person
Fine sea salt, 1 teaspoon per pound of meat
Freshly cracked Tellicherry black pepper

For the applesauce:
$^1/_2$ to $^3/_4$ pound of apples per person
Sea salt
Sugar
Butter, unsalted
Apple cider vinegar

The day before serving:

1. Season the sparerib slabs liberally with fine sea salt. Refrigerate overnight.

On the day of serving:

2. Preheat oven to 375°F.

3. Peel, core, and quarter the apples and toss with a little sea salt and a bit of sugar. Spread in a shallow roasting pan that just holds them in a crowded layer. Dot with unsalted butter, cover tightly, and bake until the apples are just starting to soften, about 30 minutes depending on the oven, the pan, and the size of the apple chunks. Uncover, raise the heat to 500°F, and return the apples to the center rack of the oven to dry out and color.

4. Once the tips of the apples have become golden and the fruit is very tender, remove from the oven, scrape into a warm bowl, stir into a chunky mash, and taste. Season with more salt and sugar to taste, and add a final splash of apple cider vinegar to brighten the flavor.

5. Preheat or reduce oven temperature to 475°F. Just before roasting, sprinkle the spareribs generously with Tellicherry pepper. Place on a heavy baking sheet, bone side up, and roast about 40 minutes until crispy, turning them over after 20 minutes. Carve into individual bones and pile on a platter accompanied by a deep bowl of the warm applesauce.

Chef's Recommendation: big red Rhône wine

Fritto Misto of Artichokes, Fennel & Lemon

SERVES 4 TO 6

Vegetable oil for frying

4 pounds baby artichokes, trimmed and quartered

Salt and pepper

2 lemons, sliced thin in rounds

1 head fennel, trimmed, cut in half, cored, and thinly shaved with a sharp
knife or mandoline

½ pound rice flour

1 bunch Italian parsley, large stems removed

½ pound Parmesan, thinly shaved

2 cups Aïoli (see sidebar on page 154)

1. Fill a large, heavy pot halfway full of vegetable oil. Heat the frying oil
   to 300°F. Be sure to wear long sleeves and be very careful that the
   vegetables are not wet when you put them into the oil. Carefully
   immerse the quartered artichokes in the hot oil and fry for about 7 to
   8 minutes. Remove from the oil and place on towels to cool and drain.
   Do not allow the artichokes to brown at all. If they begin to brown,
   remove them from the oil, reduce the oil temperature, and immerse
   again to finish.

2. Once the artichokes have cooled completely, raise the temperature of
   the oil to 340°F to 350°F. Immerse the artichokes in the hot oil, gently
   stirring until they are golden brown. Remove immediately and place on
   dry towels to drain. Sprinkle immediately with salt and pepper.

3. Quickly, before the artichokes cool, dust the lemon slices and shaved
   fennel thoroughly with rice flour, shake off excess flour, and place them
   in the hot oil—adding the lemons just a few seconds ahead of the fennel.
   Gently stir until they are nearly brown. Toss in the parsley leaves for
   about 20 seconds and remove everything from the fryer. Season with
   salt and pepper and toss together with the hot artichokes.

4. Arrange the fried vegetables in a pile and sprinkle liberally with shaved
   Parmesan. Serve hot with Aïoli for dipping.

Chef's Recommendation: dry Mourvedre rosé or champagne

**Restaurant
LuLu**
San Francisco
Jody Denton
Chef/Partner

Heat broiler. Place whole peppers in a single layer on a broiler pan lined with aluminum foil. Broil, turning peppers often until completely charred (skin black and blistered). Remove and immediately place in a bowl; cover tightly with a dish or towel. After a few moments and when just cool enough to handle, scrape the charred skin with a paring knife. Some black bits can remain. Do not wash! Working over a bowl to catch the juices, remove stems, split in half, and remove the thick inside membranes and seeds.

Lalime's
Berkeley
Frances Wilson
Executive Chef

Roasted Gypsy Pepper, Ronde de Nice Squash & Toscano Cheese Bread Pudding

SERVES 6

1 tablespoon virgin olive oil
3 Ronde de Nice squash or 1½ pounds zucchini, washed and sliced
1 large clove garlic, finely minced
4 gypsy peppers, roasted, peeled, and cut into ½-inch slices (if you can't find gypsy peppers, use a thick-walled, sweet red pepper)
1 teaspoon fresh marjoram, finely chopped
Salt and freshly ground black pepper to taste
3 eggs
1 cup heavy cream or whole milk
Pinch of mace
¾-pound loaf rustic white bread, crusts removed, cut into ¼-inch slices
½ pound grated Bellwether Farms Toscano cheese

1. Preheat oven to 350°F.

2. In a hot pan, heat the olive oil; add the squash and garlic. Sauté until the squash is cooked but still al dente, about 4 minutes. When cool, mix with the roasted, peeled peppers and the marjoram. Season with salt and pepper.

3. Brush an ovenproof 8x8-inch dish with olive oil. Whisk the eggs lightly. Add the cream, salt, pepper, and mace. One at a time, dip the slices of bread in the egg mixture and place in the dish, forming one layer. Cover the bread with a layer of the vegetables and then with a layer of the grated cheese. Make three more layers: egg-coated bread, vegetables, and cheese (reserve some cheese to sprinkle on top of the finished pudding), and then top with another layer of bread. Pour the remaining egg mixture over this final layer.

4. Cover the dish first with parchment paper and then with aluminum foil. Place the dish in a larger ovenproof dish and fill the outside dish with hot water until it reaches one-third the height of the 8x8-inch dish. Bake in the oven for 1 hour until the custard is firm to the touch. Remove the foil and parchment, sprinkle the top with the reserved cheese, and return to the oven, baking until the cheese melts and browns. Serve hot.

Chef's Recommendation: Chardonnay Dehlinger, Russian River 1997

Smoked Goat Cheddar & White Corn Chowder

MAKES 8 HEARTY 10-OUNCE SERVINGS

1 pound or 2 large Yukon Gold potatoes, peeled and diced

8 tablespoons (one stick) sweet butter

3 carrots, finely chopped

3 ribs of celery, finely chopped

2 large cloves of garlic, crushed

1 medium onion, finely chopped

5 ears of white corn kernels to make 3 cups

2 tablespoons flour

½ cup dry white wine

2 cups vegetable stock

5 cups light cream (use less cream and more vegetable stock if you wish)

1 red bell pepper, cored, seeded, and chopped

8 ounces Redwood Hill smoked goat cheddar, grated

Salt and freshly ground white pepper to taste

2 tablespoons finely minced parsley

1. Bring a pot of water to a boil and add the potatoes. Cook until just tender, about 8 minutes. Drain and set aside.

2. Melt the butter in a heavy saucepan; add the carrots, celery, garlic, and onion. Sauté over medium heat until the garlic is soft and the onions translucent, about 5 minutes (do not brown). Add the corn, stir well, and cook 2 minutes. Gradually add the flour, a little at a time, stirring, and cook about 2 minutes until the vegetables are fully coated. Add the wine and vegetable stock, stirring well and incorporating any bits on the bottom and sides of the pan. Bring to a boil and slowly add the cream, stirring constantly. Return to the boiling point, reduce the heat, and simmer for 15 to 20 minutes until the vegetables are soft. Do not let the soup boil. Add the potatoes and red pepper. (You can make the soup this far if you wish to make it ahead. Add the cheese only when ready to serve.)

3. Add the grated goat cheese, and season with salt and pepper to taste. Heat the soup over low heat until the cheese melts. Do not let the soup come to a boil, because the cheese may break up and separate. Serve hot, sprinkled with minced parsley.

Lalime's
Berkeley
Frances Wilson
Executive Chef

Roasted Potatoes & Red Onions

SERVES 8

The potatoes in this recipe are first par cooked, then browned and crisped in olive oil in a skillet on top of the stove. The red onions are also briefly blanched in boiling water, drained, and added to the potatoes at the finish. Choose potatoes such as Red Rose, Finnish, or Yukon Gold.

3½ pounds potatoes, peeled and cut into 1-inch chunks

½ gallon water

1½ tablespoon kosher salt

1 large red onion, peeled, cored, and cut into 8 wedges

¼ cup olive oil

1 teaspoon freshly ground pepper

2 tablespoons parsley, coarsely chopped

1. Place the potatoes in a large pot and add the water and 1 tablespoon of the salt. Be sure the water covers the potatoes. Bring to a boil, and then reduce the heat to a simmer. Cook the potatoes until tender, about 12 to 15 minutes.

2. Remove the cooked potatoes from the water by using a slotted spoon, and put them in a colander. Bring the potato water back to a boil and add the red onions. Cook the onions for 2 minutes and then drain them in a separate colander.

3. Place the potatoes in a large bowl and toss them with the olive oil, the remaining ½ tablespoon of salt, and the black pepper. Heat a heavy-bottomed skillet over high heat and add the seasoned potatoes. Brown the potatoes well, turning them often to be sure that all sides brown. (You may need to add a little more olive oil to achieve this.) When the potatoes are well browned, add the onions and continue to toss the two together until the onions are warmed. Add the parsley and serve.

This dish is an excellent accompaniment to Shoulder of Lamb Braised in Chianti (see page 26).

Oliveto
Oakland
Paul Bertolli
Chef/Owner

Crostini with Warm Cannellini Beans & Wilted Green Gulch Chard

SERVES 6 GENEROUSLY

1 cup dried cannellini beans, about 6 ounces

4 cups water

1 bay leaf

2 fresh sage leaves or thyme sprigs

6 to 8 tablespoons extra virgin olive oil

Salt and freshly ground black pepper

3 large garlic cloves, finely chopped

6 cups green chard or kale leaves, coarsely chopped

1 to 2 tablespoons sherry or red wine vinegar

12 thick slices sourdough bread

1. Rinse, sort, and soak beans overnight in about 2 inches of water. Drain the soaked beans and rinse well. Pour into a saucepan with the water, bay leaf, and sage or thyme. Bring to a boil. Reduce the heat, and simmer, uncovered, until the beans are very soft, 35 to 40 minutes, skimming foam as it forms. Remove the herbs and bay leaf; drain the beans, reserving the cooking liquid. Pour ⅓ cup of the liquid back into the beans and mash with a fork or potato masher. Season the warm beans with 2 tablespoons of the olive oil, ½ teaspoon salt (or more to taste), a sprinkling of pepper, and garlic to taste.

2. Heat 1 to 2 tablespoons of the olive oil in a large skillet. Add the greens, sprinkle with salt and pepper, and cook over medium heat while tossing with tongs to keep them from sticking to the pan. Add a little of the reserved cooking water to the pan, if needed. When the greens have wilted, sprinkle with 1 tablespoon of the vinegar, remove from the pan, and drain. Season with salt, pepper, and vinegar to taste. Set aside, but loosely cover to keep warm.

3. Combine the remaining 3 or 4 tablespoons of olive oil with the last of the garlic, and brush generously over the sliced bread. Grill or toast the bread, spread with the warm beans, and heap the wilted greens on top.

Chef's Recommendation: crisp Sauvignon Blanc from New Zealand or its more-smoky, mineral counterpart from the Loire Valley, such as a Sancerre or Pouilly Fumé

Extra virgin olive oil, garlic, and sherry vinegar are the flavors that set this rustic dish apart. Cannellini beans are a favorite here, but any large white bean will do: giant lima, great Northern, and sweet white runner (also called emergo) beans are equally delicious.

greens

Greens
San Francisco
Annie Somerville
Executive Chef

Baked Apple with Cream Cheese, Walnuts & Currants
with Apple Cider Cream

SERVES 4

1½ cups apple cider

Juice of 1 lemon

Juice of 1 orange

5 tablespoons firmly packed light brown sugar

⅛ teaspoon ground cinnamon

6 tablespoons softened cream cheese

⅓ cup walnut pieces

1 tablespoon maple syrup

2 tablespoons currants

4 baking apples (such as Granny Smith or Winesap)

Apple Cider Cream (see sidebar)

1. Preheat oven to 400°F.

2. In a small saucepan, combine the cider, lemon juice, orange juice, 2 tablespoons of the brown sugar, and cinnamon. Place on high heat and bring to a boil. Stirring frequently, continue boiling until the liquid is reduced to 1 cup, about 45 minutes. Remove from heat and set aside.

3. In a small bowl, combine the remaining 3 tablespoons of brown sugar, the cream cheese, walnuts, maple syrup, and currants. Mix well.

4. Core the apples, leaving the bottom of each intact. Peel each apple ⅓ of the way down from the top and fill it with the walnut mixture. Place the filled apples in a 2-quart baking dish. Pour the cider reduction into the dish. Bake for 30 to 40 minutes or until tender, basting occasionally.

5. To serve, put a few tablespoons of Apple Cider Cream into each bowl and place an apple on the cream. Top each apple with a drizzle of the pan juices.

Chef's Recommendation: Riesling Late Harvest Cluster Select Navarro, Anderson Valley

Lark Creek Inn
Larkspur
Bradley Ogden
Chef/Co-owner

Apple Cider Cream

makes 1 cup

1¹/₂ cups apple cider

1 tablespoon apple brandy

¹/₂ tart apple, cored and cut into 1-inch pieces

¹/₃ cup heavy cream

In a medium-size stainless steel saucepan, combine the cider, the brandy, and the apple. Bring the mixture to a boil over medium-high heat. Continue boiling, stirring occasionally, until the liquid is reduced to ³/₄ cup, about 10 minutes.

Remove the pan from the heat and stir the cream into the reduced cider. Return the pan to the heat and cook, stirring often, over medium heat until the sauce has reduced to 1 cup, about 3 minutes. Remove from the heat, strain, and set aside.

**Local Foods
Local Flavors**

Straus Family Creamery *is a small, family-owned dairy farm nestled in the beautiful rolling hills of western Marin County. The Straus family, which has been farming there for more than 50 years, is committed to producing milk and dairy products that are organic and healthful and to developing sustainable, environmentally sound practices in farming. Known for their cream-top milk in glass bottles, the creamery's products include milk, butter, cream, and cheese.*

Basil Oil

1 bunch basil

1 cup extra virgin olive oil

Blanch basil in boiling salted water. Immerse in ice water, remove, and squeeze out excess water. Place the basil and olive oil in a blender and blend until smooth. Let stand 2 hours and strain.

Butternut Squash, Cabbage & Pancetta Risotto with Basil Oil

SERVES 8

2 sticks butter

1/2 medium-size sweet onion, diced

1 pound Arborio rice

3/4 cup white wine

2 quarts chicken stock

1/2 pound butternut squash, peeled, diced, and steamed until tender

4 ounces Parmesan cheese, grated

Salt and pepper to taste

4 ounces pancetta bacon, diced

1/2 pound savoy cabbage, sliced in very thin strips

1/4 cup Basil Oil (see sidebar)

1. In a medium-size saucepan, melt 1 stick of butter over low heat. Add the sweet onion and cook until translucent. Add the rice and stir to coat evenly with butter. Add the white wine and boil until it is reduced by two-thirds.

2. Bring the chicken stock to a boil, turn down the heat, and keep it at a slow simmer. Add the chicken stock to the rice by the cupful, stirring constantly and allowing the stock to be absorbed before you add the next cup. When all of the stock has been added and absorbed, add the diced butternut squash, the remaining stick of butter, and the Parmesan cheese. Remove from heat and season with salt and pepper. Let stand.

3. Heat the pancetta slowly in a small frying pan over low heat to render (or melt) the fat. Then add the cabbage and cook in the fat until tender. Season with salt and pepper.

4. To serve, place 6 to 8 ounces risotto in each bowl, garnish with cabbage, and drizzle with basil oil.

Chef's Recommendation: Chardonnay, Stone Street 1996

❑❑ PARK GRILL ❑❑

**Park Hyatt
San Francisco**
San Francisco
George Cronk
Former Executive
Chef

Twice-Baked Parmesan Soufflé
with Romano Beans & French Butter Pears

SERVES 6

9 tablespoons unsalted butter

³/₄ cup flour

2 cups milk

¹/₂ cup grated Parmesan (preferably Reggiano)

2 teaspoons salt

4 extra-large eggs, separated

¹/₂ pound Romano beans (Italian flat beans)

2 small ripe pears, preferably Pettigrew Farms French Butter pears

Large handful arugula, washed and trimmed

Vinaigrette (see sidebar)

1. Preheat oven to 375°F.

2. Melt butter in medium-size saucepan. Whisk in flour and cook, whisking for 3 minutes over medium heat. Slowly add milk in a steady stream, whisking continuously; cook until mixture reaches the boiling point, but do not boil. Cook for 2 more minutes, whisking. Remove from heat and pour into a bowl. Let cool. Stir in cheese, salt, and egg yolks.

3. Whip egg whites until firm but not stiff; fold into cheese mixture. Divide evenly among 6 buttered ramekins. Place ramekins in a pan of hot water that reaches one-third of the way up the sides of the ramekins. Bake for 20 to 25 minutes until soufflés puff up, begin to brown, and are firm to the touch. Remove from oven and cool on a rack. When cool, run a knife around the edges of the ramekins and gently unmold. Place soufflés on buttered parchment paper on a baking sheet.

4. Cook Romano beans in rapidly boiling salted water until tender. Cool and cut diagonally into 2-inch pieces.

5. Cut pears in half. Remove cores and slice thinly.

6. Increase oven to 400°F. Bake soufflés until brown and puffed, 8 to 10 minutes. While soufflés are baking, toss together beans, pears, arugula, and vinaigrette. Arrange salad on 6 plates. Top each with a hot soufflé.

Chef's Recommendation: Sancerre Menetou-Salon

Vinaigrette

¹/₄ cup extra virgin olive oil

2 tablespoons sherry vinegar

1 shallot, minced

¹/₂ teaspoon salt

¹/₄ teaspoon freshly ground black pepper

Combine olive oil, vinegar, shallot, and salt and pepper to taste.

Rivoli
Berkeley
Wendy Brucker
Chef/Owner

Where to find chefs who are Cooking Fresh

DAN & KATHLEEN BERMAN
Mixx
135 Fourth Street
Santa Rosa, CA 95401
707-573-1344

Mixx proprietors and chefs Dan and Kathleen Berman offer fresh, regional eclectic cuisine featuring a local mix of fresh Sonoma County produce, meats, and dairy products with their award-winning wine and dessert lists.

PAUL BERTOLLI
Oliveto
5655 College Avenue
Oakland, CA 94618
510-547-5356

Oliveto's Paul Bertolli has mastered age-old techniques that rely on the use of the freshest ingredients, an appreciation of their particular qualities, and the skillful coaxing of their best possible flavors. Nestled in Oakland's distinctive and charming Rockridge neighborhood.

WENDY BRUCKER
Rivoli
1539 Solano Avenue
Berkeley, CA 94707
510-526-2542

With its contemporary American food and casual but elegant dining, Rivoli and Wendy Brucker specialize in preparing local and seasonal menus using predominantly organic ingredients, natural meats and poultry, and local and seasonal seafood.

JESSE COOL
Flea Street Café
3607 Alameda de las Pulgas
Menlo Park, CA 94025
650-854-1226

With Jesse Cool's emphasis on seasonal and organic ingredients, Flea Street Café is a casually elegant restaurant appropriate for both business and private dining.

GEORGE CRONK
Park Grill
Park Hyatt San Francisco
333 Battery Street
San Francisco, CA 94111
415-392-1234

Award-winning Park Grill has produced a popular, private club atmosphere to showcase Chef George Cronk's menus of delicious California cuisine. Menus are continually updated to present unique selections reflecting the freshest local and seasonal produce and seafood.

GARY DANKO
Gary Danko
800 North Point at Hyde Street
San Francisco, CA 94109
415-749-2060

Award-winning chef Gary Danko's distinctive culinary style combines the sophisticated refinement of classical cuisine with the satisfying exuberance of traditional cooking.

JODY DENTON
Restaurant LuLu
816 Folsom Street
San Francisco, CA 94107
415-495-5775

Restaurant LuLu's executive chef and partner Jody Denton prepares simple, earthy, and varied cuisine of Provence and the French Riviera. Located in San Francisco's South Market district in a beautifully renovated, vintage 1910 warehouse.

ANNE GINGRASS
Hawthorne Lane
22 Hawthorne Street
San Francisco, CA 94105
415-777-9779

The menus at Hawthorne Lane are built around the bounty of northern California's farms, ranches, dairies, and waters. Chef Anne Gingrass's distinctive style combines strong flavors with contrasting textures and temperatures to create dishes that are satisfying and memorable.

REED HEARON
Rose Pistola
532 Columbus Avenue
San Francisco, CA 94133
415-399-0499

Reed Hearon's Rose Pistola features a variety of tastes and shared pleasures by lending itself to family-style dining. The food is inspired by the cooking of the area's oldest residents, most of whom hail from Genoa and the Ligurina coast.

DAVID KINCH
Restaurant Sent Sovi
14583 Big Basin Way
Saratoga, CA 95070
408-867-3110

The small, intimate, French-California Restaurant Sent Sovi is a culinary gem located in Saratoga. David Kinch's small, ever-changing menu offers both à la carte and six-course tasting menus that rely on local farmers and wineries for the freshest, most up-to-the-minute flavors possible.

NANCY OAKES
Boulevard
One Mission Street
San Francisco, CA 94105
415-543-6084

At Boulevard, Chef Nancy Oakes assimilates a range of ethnic influences into her cooking, including Asian, Mediterranean, and Latin. Classic French sensibilities and fresh, flavorful ingredients form the backbone of her seasonal and modern American menu.

BRADLEY OGDEN
Lark Creek Inn
234 Magnolia Avenue
Larkspur, CA 94939
415-924-7766

Located in picturesque Larkspur, Lark Creek Inn and Bradley Ogden have been hailed for their seasonal, farm-fresh American fare.

DANIEL PATTERSON
Elisabeth Daniel
550 Washington Street
San Francisco, CA 94111
415-397-6129

Chef Daniel Patterson and wife Elisabeth Ramsey offer a classically French progression of courses using fresh, organic ingredients. Elisabeth Daniel is located in San Francisco's historic Jackson Square neighborhood.

MICHAEL QUIGLEY
Cafe Lolo
620 Fifth Street
Santa Rosa, CA 95404
707-576-7822

Nationally acclaimed Cafe Lolo is a small, intimate café serving Michael Quigley's California wine-country cuisine and featuring local and seasonal ingredients.

JUDY RODGERS
Zuni
1658 Market Street
San Francisco, CA 94102
415-552-2522

An animated, bohemian-spirited restaurant, Zuni and Judy Rodgers feature inspired dishes made with the freshest ingredients possible.

ANNIE SOMERVILLE
Greens
Fort Mason, Building A
San Francisco, CA 94123
415-771-6222

A world-renowned vegetarian restaurant, Greens has been delighting patrons with its fresh, meatless cuisine for over 20 years. Annie Somerville is a well-known vegetarian chef and cookbook author.

RALPH TINGLE
Bistro Ralph
109 Plaza Street
Healdsburg, CA 95448
707-433-1380

Located in Healdsburg, Bistro Ralph is small, slightly loud, and absolutely unpretentious. It's a nice cross between city and country with Ralph Tingle's menu to match.

ERIC TUCKER
Millennium
246 McAllister Street
San Francisco, CA 94102
415-487-9800

A fine-dining, vegetarian restaurant, Millennium specializes in Eric Tucker's eclectic, world cuisine, artfully presented and emphasizing local and organic produce, grains, and beans.

THOMAS VINOLUS
Bittersweet Bistro
787 Rio del Mar Boulevard
Aptos, CA 95003
831-662-9799

Housed in the 100-year-old former Deer Park Tavern in Rio del Mar, Bittersweet Bistro and Thomas Vinolus feature American bistro dining with Mediterranean influences.

FRANCES WILSON
Lalime's
1329 Gilman Street
Berkeley, CA 94706
510-527-9838

With the soul of a fine-dining restaurant and the heart of a family sharing a meal, Lalime's features Frances Wilson's California-Mediterranean cuisine prix-fixe dinners every night as well as à la carte menus.

Contact Information

AUTHORS

MARION LONG BOWLAN
Executive Director
PA Farm Link
2708 A North Colebrook Road
Manheim, PA 17545
717-664-7077
Fax 717-664-7078
pafarmlink@reelrose.net

JIM COCHRAN
Swanton Berry Farm
P.O. Box 308
Davenport, CA 95017
831-425-8919
www.swantonberry.com

TIM COHEN-MITCHELL
Co-Chair, Board of Directors
Valley Trade Connection
Greenfield, MA 01301
413-774-7204
www.valleydollars.org

STUART DICKSON
Stone Free Farm
P.O. Box 1437
Watsonville, CA 95077
831-726-5111

GAIL FEENSTRA
Food Systems Coordinator
Sustainable Agriculture Research
   and Education Program
University of California
One Shields Avenue
Davis, CA 95616
530-752-8408

K. DUN GIFFORD
Founder and President
Oldways Preservation
   & Exchange Trust
25 First Street
Cambridge, MA 02141
617-621-3000
www.oldwayspt.org

TERRY GIPS
President
Sustainability Associates
2584 Upton Avenue South
Minneapolis, MN 55405
612-374-4765

TOM HALLER
Director Emeritus
Community Alliance with
   Family Farmers
P.O. Box 363
Davis, CA 95617
530-756-8518

ELIZABETH HENDERSON
Peacework Organic Farm
2218 Welcher Road
Newark, NY 14513
315-331-9029

PETER JARET
Medical Journalist
Contributing Editor
   to *Health* Magazine
609 C Street
Petaluma, CA 94952

SIBELLA KRAUS
Center for Urban Education
   about Sustainable Agriculture
2000 Van Ness, Suite 512
San Francisco, CA 94109
415-353-5650
www.ferryplazafarmersmarket.com

MARK LIPSON
Organic Farming Research
   Foundation
P.O. Box 440
Santa Cruz, CA 95061
408-426-6606
research@ofrf.org

MOTHERS & OTHERS
40 West 20th Street, 9th Floor
New York, NY 10011
212-242-0010
shoppers@mothers.org
www.mothers.org/mothers

PAUL MULLER
Full Belly Farm
P.O. Box 222
Guinda, CA 95637
530-796-2214

NELL NEWMAN
Newman's Own Organics
P.O. Box 2098
Aptos, CA 95001
408-685-2866

DAVID PIMENTEL
Professor of Ecology
   and Agricultural Sciences
Cornell University
5126 Comstock Hall
Ithaca, NY 14853
607-255-2212
dp18@cornell.edu

BERNADINE PRINCE
American Farmland Trust
1200 18th Street NW, Suite 800
Washington, DC 20036
202-331-7300

HOPE SHAND
Research Director
Rural Advancement Foundation
   International
P.O. Box 640
Pittsboro, NC 27312
919-542-1396
www.rafi.org

MICHAEL SHUMAN
Author, *Going Local: Creating Self-Reliant Communities in a Global Era* (Free Press)
Director, Institute for Economic Education and Entrepreneurship for the Village Foundation
3713 Warren Street NW
Washington, DC 20016
202-364-4051
www.progressivepubs.com

JOEL SIMMONS
President
EarthWorks
P.O. Box 278K
Martins Creek, PA 18063
800-732-8873
http://www.soilfirst.com

CARL SMITH
Director of Publications
Foundation for Advancements in Science and Education
4801 Wilshire Blvd., Suite 215
Los Angeles, CA 90010
323-937-9911

GARY L. VALEN
Director of Sustainable Agriculture
Humane Society of the United States
2100 L Street NW
Washington, DC 20037
202-452-1100
www.hsus.org

DENESSE WILLEY
T&D Willey Farms
13886 Road 20
Madera, CA 93637
559-673-9058
denesse@tdwilleyfarms.com

FARMS & FARM PRODUCTS

BELLWETHER FARMS
P.O. Box 299
Valley Ford, CA 94972
888-527-8606
Fax: 707-763-2443
www.bellwethercheese.com
(not open to public)
see page 119

COWGIRL CREAMERY
at Tomales Bay Foods:
80 Fourth Street
Point Reyes Station, CA 94956
415-663-9335
at Artisan Cheese:
2413 California Street
San Francisco, CA 94115
415-929-8610
www.cowgirlcreamery.com
see page 29

DAVERO
707-431-8000
Fax: 707-433-5780
info@davero.com
www.davero.com
(not open to public)
see page 85

FULL BELLY FARM
P.O. Box 222
Guinda, CA 95637
530-796-2214
see page 5

LAURA CHENEL'S CHÈVRE
4310 Fremont Drive
Sonoma, CA 95476
707-996-4477
Fax: 707-996-1816
(not open to the public)
see page 157

NATIVE KJALII FOODS
P.O. Box 1508
San Leandro, CA 94577
888-229-0123
customer-service@sfsalsa.com
www.sfsalsa.com
see page 37

NICK SCIABICA & SONS
P.O. Box 1246
Modesto, CA 95353-1246
800-551-9612, extension 23
Fax: 209-524-5367
www.sciabica.com
see page 149

NIMAN RANCH
1025 East 12th Street
Oakland, CA 94606
510-808-0330
info@nimanranch.com
www.nimanranch.com
see page 111

PETALUMA POULTRY
P.O. Box 7368
Petaluma, CA 94955-7368
707-763-1904
Fax: 707-763-3924
www.healthychickenchoices.com
see page 123

REDWOOD HILL FARM
10855 Occidental Road
Sebastopol, CA 95472
707-823-8250
Fax: 707-823-6976
contact@redwoodhill.com
www.redwoodhill.com
(by appointment only)
see page 77

STONE FREE FARM
P.O. Box 1437
Watsonville, CA 95077
831-726-5111
Fax 831-726-5110
see page 89

**STRAUS FAMILY
CREAMERY**
P.O. Box 768
Marshall, CA 94940
415-663-5464
family@strausmilk.com
www.strausmilk.com
see page 167

SWANTON BERRY FARM
P.O. Box 308
Davenport, CA 95017
831-425-8919
www.swantonberry.com
see page 129

T&D WILLEY FARMS
13886 Road 20
Madera, CA 93637
559-673-9058
www.tdwilleyfarms.com
see page 49

ORGANIZATIONS

**AMERICAN FARMLAND
TRUST**
1200 18th Street NW, Suite 800
Washington, DC 20036
202-331-7300
info@farmland.org
http://www.farmland.org
see page 131

**BERKELEY REGION
EXCHANGE AND
DEVELOPMENT**
P.O. Box 3973
Berkeley, CA 94703
510-704-5247
bkbread@pacbell.net
http://home.pacbell.net/bkbread
see page 12

**CALIFORNIA CLEAN
GROWERS ASSOCIATION**
calclean@californiaclean.com
http://www.californiaclean.com/
see page 55

**CALIFORNIANS FOR
PESTICIDE REFORM**
49 Powell Street, Suite 530
San Francisco, CA 94102
415-981-3939
Fax 415-981-2727
pests@igc.org
http://www.igc.org/cpr
see page 139

**CENTER FOR URBAN
EDUCATION ABOUT
SUSTAINABLE
AGRICULTURE**
2000 Van Ness, Suite 512
San Francisco, CA 94109
415-353-5650
Fax 415-440-2206
www.ferryplazafarmersmarket.com
see page xiv

CHEF'S COLLABORATIVE
282 Moody Street • Suite 207
Waltham, MA 02453
781-736-0635
Fax 781-642-0307
cc2000@chefnet.com
see page 53

**CHEZ PANISSE
FOUNDATION**
1517 Shattuck Avenue
Berkeley, CA 94709
510-843-3811
see page 96

**COMMUNITY ALLIANCE
WITH FAMILY FARMERS**
P.O. Box 363
Davis, CA 95617
530-756-8518
Fax 530-756-7857
http://www.caff.org/
see page 6

GREENBELT ALLIANCE
530 Bush Street, #303
San Francisco, CA 94108
415-398-3730
Fax 415-398-6530
http://www.greenbelt.org
see page 134

MOTHERS & OTHERS
40 West 20th Street, 9th Floor
New York, NY 10011
212-242-0010
shoppers@mothers.org
http://www.mothers.org/mothers
see page 56

**ORGANIC FARMING
RESEARCH FOUNDATION**
P.O. Box 440
Santa Cruz, CA 95061
831-426-6606
Fax 831-426-6670
research@ofrf.org
http://www.ofrf.org
see page 51

SELECT SONOMA COUNTY
5000 Roberts Lake Road, Suite A
Rohnert Park, CA 94928
707-586-2233
Fax 707-586-3547
info@sonomagrown.com
http://www.sonomagrown.com
see page 91

SLOW FOOD
P.O. Box 1737
New York, NY 10021
1-877-756-9366
www.slowfood.com
see page 9

**SONOMA COUNTY FARM
TRAILS**
P.O. Box 6032
Santa Rosa, CA 95406
707-571-8288
Fax 707-571-7719
farmtrails@farmtrails.org
http://www.farmtrails.org
see page 93

Notes

FOOD SAFETY

Raw Eggs

The consumption of raw eggs is the subject of much debate. Your chances of getting sick from eating raw eggs depends to a large extent on the quality of the eggs and your own susceptibility to illness. If you do use raw eggs, be sure that they are very fresh. Raw eggs and sauces made with raw eggs should be kept refrigerated. Never serve raw eggs to young children, the elderly, or people with compromised immune systems.

Aïoli is basically a garlic-flavored mayonnaise. It is more delicious because it is made with olive oil and lemon juice, but if you are concerned about the use of raw eggs, you can approximate the flavor by adding pureed garlic to prepared mayonnaise and seasoning with salt and pepper.

Recommended Internal Temperatures for Roasted Meats

Poultry: 180°F
Beef, lamb & pork: 160°F

SEASONAL AVAILABILITY

The Seasonal Availability chart on page 136 is based on the Crop Timetable from Eatwell Farm's Web site (www.eatwell.com). Additions were made based on Chez Panisse's Forager's Diary and comments from Stuart Dickson of Stonefree Farm and Jim Cochran of Swanton Berry Farm. Additional comments came from Allstate Packers, the Apple Farm, Benzler Farms, Green Cedar Farm, La Rocca Vineyards, Riverview Orchard, Timber Crest Farms, and Todd Ranch.

At any given time, the availability of local produce will vary depending on the weather. Retailers' supplies of local produce will also vary depending on the geographic and climatic range of the local farmers who supply those retailers.

For a full selection of locally grown produce, visit your local farmers market, join a CSA, or shop at stores—like Real Foods and Rainbow in San Francisco—that specialize in local produce.

For a list of what is currently available at the farmers market, visit the Ferry Plaza Web site at www.ferryplazafarmersmarket.com.

RESOURCES FOR STORAGE & PRESERVATION

Eat Fresh, Stay Healthy
by Tony Tantillo & Sam Gugino

Fresh from the Farmers' Market
by Janet Fletcher

The Green Kitchen Handbook
by Annie Berthold-Bond

Keeping Food Fresh
by The Gardeners & Farmers of Terre Vivante

Parsley, Peppers, Potatoes & Peas
by Pat Katz

Putting Food By (4th Edition)
by Janet Greene, Ruth Hertzberg & Beatrice Vaughan

Stocking Up (3rd Edition)
by Carol Hupping

Index to Ingredients

aïoli, 154
apple(s):
    baked, with cream cheese, walnuts & currants
        with cider cream, 166
    butternut squash bisque, 146
    celeriac &, soup with St. George cheese toasts,
        43
    cider cream, 167
    pork chops braised with red cabbage &, 15
    salt & pepper spareribs with roasted applesauce,
        160
    stuffed caramelized tomatoes with vanilla
        ice cream, 120
    tarte tatin with cider sauce, 155
artichokes:
    a stew of, butternut squash & clams in a lemon,
        garlic, saffron, oregano sauce, 158
    feuilletée of morels, roasted fennel & fava beans
        with an asparagus beurre blanc, 76
    fritto misto of, fennel & lemon, 161
    petite aïoli: ahi tuna, potato & vegetable salad,
        154
    ragout of spring vegetables with aged sherry
        vinegar & green olive oil, 84
    shaved raw, fava beans & Parmesan, 68
    spring vegetable & lemongrass stew with
        poached grouper, 59
    torta (frittata), 62
arugula:
    chopped salad, 105
    creamer potato & caramelized onion pizza with
        fontina cheese & fresh, 144
    farfalle pasta with roasted pumpkin & a pumpkin
        seed-ancho chili pesto, 159
    frisee &, salad with spring chanterelles, green
        garlic, italian parsley & croutons, 60
    late summer salad: figs & melon with goat
        cheese & citrus vinaigrette, 99
    salad with raw sweet corn & sweet 100
        tomatoes, 102
    twice-baked Parmesan soufflé with romano
        beans & french butter pears, 169
asparagus:
    & buttermilk soup, 73
    crab &, soup with green onions & cilantro, 64
    feuilletée of morels, artichokes, roasted fennel &
        fava beans with an, beurre blanc, 76
    grilled, with Meyer lemon vinaigrette & shaved
        Bellwether Pecorino Pepato, 58
    Provençal vegetable ragout, 72
    salad with Meyer lemon vinaigrette, 79
    southwestern, corn & tomatillo soup, 69
    tempura-fried, spears, 65
    with balsamic syrup & Parmigiano-Reggiano, 67

balsamic glaze, 31
basil(s):
    artichoke torta (frittata), 62
    coriander-cured lamb with dried-cherry-Zinfandel
        sauce &, mashed potatoes, 44
    creamed corn & marinated tomatoes with
        assorted, 116
    mashed potatoes, 45
    oil, 168
beans:
    chicken pot pie, 122
    cooking fresh pod, 100
    pan roast chicken breasts with summer
        succotash, 100
    petite aïoli: ahi tuna, potato & vegetable salad,
        154
    twice-baked Parmesan soufflé with romano, &
        french butter pears, 169
beans (dried):
    crostini with warm cannellini, & wilted green
        gulch chard, 165
    winter vegetables & white bean ragout, 38
beef:
    roasted tenderloin of, with chanterelle bread
        pudding & warm treviso salad, 40
    tenderloin, preparing, 40
beets:
    many-vegetable pasta with feta cheese, 36
    ragout of spring vegetables with aged sherry
        vinegar & green olive oil, 84
berries:
    almond tart with fresh, 80
    chocolate-dipped strawberries, 80
    fresh strawberry ice cream, 81
    just-baked wild boysenberry shortcake, 83
    strawberry soup with lemon balm granita, 78
    summer-fruit shortcakes with lemon curd
        & whipped cream, 118
broccoli:
    chicken pot pie, 122
    many-vegetable pasta with feta cheese, 36
broccoli rabe:
    blanching, 114
    roasted salmon with oven-dried cherry tomatoes,
        shiitake mushrooms &, 114
    winter sweet potato & confit of duck Napoleon
        with rapini,, 16
cabbage:
    butternut squash, & pancetta risotto with basil
        oil, 168
    many-vegetable pasta with feta cheese, 36
    pork chops braised with red, & apples, 15

carrots:
    chicken pot pie, 122
    many-vegetable pasta with feta cheese, 36
    Provençal vegetable ragout, 72
    ragout of spring vegetables with aged sherry
        vinegar & green olive oil, 84
cashew cream, 69
cauliflower:
    chicken pot pie, 122
    many-vegetable pasta with feta cheese, 36
celery root (celeriac):
    & apple soup with St. George cheese toasts, 43
    chips, 32
    ragout of spring vegetables with aged sherry
        vinegar & green olive oil, 84
    risotto cakes with forest mushrooms &, chips, 32
chanterelles, see mushrooms
chard:
    chicken pot pie, 122
    crostini with warm cannellini beans & wilted
        green gulch, 165
cheese:
    asparagus with balsamic syrup & Parmigiano-
        Reggiano, 67
    celeriac & apple soup with St. George, toasts, 43
    creamer potato & caramelized onion pizza with
        fontina, & fresh arugula, 144
    grilled asparagus with Meyer lemon vinaigrette
        & shaved Bellwether Pecorino Pepato, 58
    late summer salad: figs & melon with goat, &
        citrus vinaigrette, 99
    many-vegetable pasta with feta, 36
    Parmesan croutons, 71
    roasted acorn squash, pears & potatoes with
        Bucheron, 18
    roasted gypsy pepper, ronde de nice squash &
        Toscano, bread pudding, 162
    St. George cheese toasts, 43
    shaved raw artichokes, fava beans & Parmesan,
        68
    smoked goat cheddar & white corn chowder,
        163
    summer Mediterranean gratin, 124
    twice-baked Parmesan soufflé with romano
        beans & french butter pears, 169
    warm flan of Laura Chenel goat, with bell pepper
        puree, 153
cherry, dried, Zinfandel sauce, 45
chicken:
    pan roast, breasts with summer succotash, 100
    pot pie, 122
    roasted, with tarragon peach sauce, 61
    stock, 71
cider sauce, 155
clams, a stew of artichokes, butternut squash &,
    in a lemon, garlic, saffron, oregano sauce, 158

corn:
    arugula salad with raw sweet, & sweet
        100 tomatoes, 102
    creamed, & marinated tomatoes with assorted
        basils, 116
    grilled day boat scallops, 66
    pan roast chicken breasts with summer
        succotash, 100
    smoked goat cheddar & white, chowder, 163
    southwestern asparagus, & tomatillo soup, 69
    spoon bread, 98
    summer sweet, & Yukon Gold chowder with okra
        relish, 125
    white truffle butter, 107
    yellow,/brioche pudding with white truffle
        butter, 106
crab & asparagus soup with green onions & cilantro,
    64
cream, reducing, 153
crème anglaise, 25
duck:
    empanada stuffed with, confit & chanterelle
        mushrooms, 42
    rendered, fat, 17
    winter sweet potato & confit of, Napoleon with
        rapini, 16
eggplant:
    summer Mediterranean gratin, 124
fava beans:
    feuilletée of morels, artichokes, roasted fennel &,
        with an asparagus beurre blanc, 76
    shaved raw artichokes, & Parmesan, 68
    spring lamb chops with, -mashed potatoes, 82
fennel:
    feuilletée of morels, artichokes, roasted, & fava
        beans with an asparagus beurre blanc, 76
    fritto misto of artichokes, & lemon, 161
    grilled day boat scallops, 66
    petite aïoli: ahi tuna, potato & vegetable salad,
        154
    summer Mediterranean gratin, 124
figs, late summer salad, & melon with goat cheese &
    citrus vinaigrette, 99
fish:
    baked red snapper with tomatoes, peppers
        & onions, 103
    fresh tuna steak, 104
    fumet, 75
    grilled, with heirloom tomatoes & salsa verde,
        110
    halibut fillet with lemon-mushroom sauce, 23
    petite aïoli: ahi tuna, potato & vegetable salad,
        154
    roasted salmon with oven-dried cherry tomatoes,
        shiitake mushrooms & broccoli rabe, 114
    roasted whole sea bass with potatoes & porcini,
        156
    seared rare ahi suspended in lemon/black pepper
        gelée, 152

spicy tuna, caper, anchovy & tomato sandwiches,
    104
spring vegetable & lemongrass stew with
    poached grouper, 59
frisee:
    & arugula salad with spring chanterelles, green
        garlic, italian parsley & croutons, 60
    roasted tenderloin of beef with chanterelle bread
        pudding & warm treviso salad, 40
garlic:
    aïoli, 154
    coriander-cured lamb with dried-cherry Zinfandel
        sauce & basil mashed potatoes, 44
    frisee & arugula salad with spring chanterelles,
        green, italian parsley & croutons, 60
    roasted acorn squash, pears & potatoes with
        Bucheron cheese, 18
    sage & milk brined pork loin with cavolo nero, 20
    shoulder of lamb braised in chianti, 26
greens, dark, leafy: (see also chard, kale)
    many-vegetable pasta with feta cheese, 36
greens, salad: (see also arugula, frisee, romaine)
    asparagus salad with Meyer lemon vinaigrette,
        79
    late summer salad: figs & melon with goat
        cheese & citrus vinaigrette, 99
    pear & pomegranate salad with walnut
        vinaigrette & balsamic glaze, 31
kale:
    crostini with warm cannellini beans & wilted
        green gulch chard, 165
    many-vegetable pasta with feta cheese, 36
    sage & milk brined pork loin with cavolo nero, 20
lamb:
    coriander-cured, with dried-cherry Zinfandel
        sauce & basil mashed potatoes, 44
    meat loaf with garlic buttermilk mashed potatoes
        & sautéed chanterelles, 148
    medallions of, with sun-dried cranberries & Pinot
        Noir, 147
    shoulder of, braised in chianti, 26
    smoked, & garlic sausage with roasted red
        pepper confit & mustard sauce, 108
    spring, chops with fava-mashed potatoes, 82
leek:
    glazed oysters with, fondue, 74
    ragout of spring vegetables with aged sherry
        vinegar & green olive oil, 84
    roasted chicken with tarragon peach sauce, 61
    yellow corn/brioche pudding with white truffle
        butter, 106
lemon:
    curd, 118
    fritto misto of artichokes, fennel &, 161
    grilled asparagus with Meyer, vinaigrette &
        shaved Bellwether Pecorino Pepato, 58
    Meyer, & hazelnut meringue tart, 28
    Meyer, vinaigrette, 58, 79
melon, late summer salad: figs &, with goat cheese
    & citrus vinaigrette, 99

mushrooms:
    chicken pot pie, 122
    consommé of shiitake, & julienne vegetables, 30
    empanada stuffed with duck confit & chanterelle,
        42
    feuilletée of morels, artichokes, roasted fennel &
        fava beans with an asparagus beurre blanc,
        76
    frisee & arugula salad with spring chanterelles,
        green garlic, italian parsley & croutons, 60
    halibut fillet with lemon, sauce, 23
    lamb meat loaf with garlic buttermilk mashed
        potatoes & sautéed chanterelles, 148
    provençal vegetable ragout, 72
    risotto cakes with forest, & celery root chips, 32
    roasted salmon with oven-dried cherry tomatoes,
        shiitake, & broccoli rabe, 114
    roasted tenderloin of beef with chanterelle bread
        pudding & warm treviso salad, 40
    roasted whole sea bass with potatoes & porcini,
        156
    sautéed chanterelles, 149
    shiitake garnish, 30
mustard thyme butter, 15
nuts:
    baked apple with cream cheese, walnuts &
        currants with apple cider cream, 166
    ginger-glazed plum & walnut galette, 112
    Meyer lemon & hazelnut meringue tart, 28
    pear & pomegranate salad with walnut
        vinaigrette & balsamic glaze, 31
okra relish, 125
onions:
    baked red snapper with tomatoes, peppers &,
        103
    creamer potato & caramelized, pizza with fontina
        cheese & fresh arugula, 144
    roasted acorn squash, pears & potatoes with
        Bucheron cheese, 18
    roasted potatoes & red, 164
    summer Mediterranean gratin, 124
    winter squash soup with sweet potato pecan
        relish, 34
oysters, glazed, with leek fondue, 74
Parmesan croutons, 71
parsnip:
    many-vegetable pasta with feta cheese, 36
    puree, 22
    savory, muffins, 22
peach(es):
    galette, 115
    peeling, 117
    roasted chicken with tarragon, sauce, 61
    summer-fruit shortcakes with lemon curd &
        whipped cream, 118
    white, poached in Gewürztraminer with vanilla &
        mascarpone, 117

pear(s):
  & pomegranate salad with walnut vinaigrette
    & balsamic glaze, 31
  roasted acorn squash, & potatoes with Bucheron
    cheese, 18
  stuffed caramelized tomatoes with vanilla
    ice cream, 120
  twice-baked Parmesan soufflé with romano
    beans & french butter, 169
  winter squash, soup with tarragon cream, 19
peas:
  cooking fresh, 100
  crab & asparagus soup with green onions
    & cilantro, 64
  grilled day boat scallops, 66
  Provençal vegetable ragout, 72
pepper(s):
  baked red snapper with tomatoes, & onions, 103
  bell, puree, 153
  petite aïoli: ahi tuna, potato & vegetable salad,
    154
  pumpkin seed-ancho chili pesto, 159
  roasted gypsy, ronde de nice squash & Toscano
    cheese bread pudding, 162
  roasting, 162
  smoked goat cheddar & white corn chowder,
    163
  smoked lamb & garlic sausage with roasted red,
    confit & mustard sauce, 108
  warm flan of Laura Chenel goat cheese with bell,
    puree, 153
  winter squash soup with sweet potato pecan
    relish, 34
  winter vegetables & white bean ragout, 38
persimmon:
  pudding with crème anglaise, 24
  puree, 24
plum:
  ginger-glazed, & walnut galette, 112
  summer-fruit shortcakes with lemon curd &
    whipped cream, 118
pomegranate, pear &, salad with walnut vinaigrette
  & balsamic glaze, 31
pork:
  chops braised with red cabbage & apples, 15
  sage & milk brined, loin with cavolo nero, 20
  salt & pepper spareribs with roasted applesauce,
    160
potato(es):
  basil mashed, 45
  coriander-cured lamb with dried-cherry Zinfandel
    sauce & basil mashed, 44
  creamer, & caramelized onion pizza with fontina
    cheese & fresh arugula, 144
  deep-fried, sticks, 109
  lamb meat loaf with garlic buttermilk mashed, &
    sautéed chanterelles, 148
  many-vegetable pasta with feta cheese, 36
  petite aïoli: ahi tuna, & vegetable salad, 154

roasted acorn squash, pears &, with Bucheron
  cheese, 18
roasted, & red onions, 164
roasted whole sea bass with, & porcini, 156
smoked goat cheddar & white corn chowder,
  163
spring lamb chops with fava-mashed, 82
summer sweet corn & Yukon Gold chowder with
  okra relish, 125
pumpkin:
  cheesecake with a chocolate hazelnut crust, 150
  farfalle pasta with roasted, & a pumpkin seed-
    ancho chili pesto, 159
  roasted, 159
  seed-ancho chili pesto, 159
radicchio:
  chopped salad, 105
  grilled, with balsamic mayonnaise, 14
  roasted tenderloin of beef with chanterelle bread
    pudding & warm treviso salad, 40
romaine:
  chopped salad, 105
rutabaga:
  many-vegetable pasta with feta cheese, 36
St. George cheese toasts, 43
salsa verde, 111
sausage, smoked lamb & garlic, with roasted red
  pepper confit & mustard sauce, 108
scallops, grilled day boat, 66
shiitake, see mushrooms
simple syrup, 83
spinach:
  artichoke torta (frittata), 62
  farfalle pasta with roasted pumpkin & a pumpkin
    seed-ancho chili pesto, 159
spring vegetable soup, 70
squash:
  a stew of artichokes, butternut, & clams in a
    lemon, garlic, saffron, oregano sauce, 158
  butternut, bisque, 146
  butternut, cabbage & pancetta risotto with basil
    oil, 168
  farfalle pasta with roasted pumpkin & a pumpkin
    seed-ancho chili pesto, 159
  roasted acorn, pears & potatoes with Bucheron
    cheese, 18
  roasted gypsy pepper, ronde de nice, & Toscano
    cheese bread pudding, 162
  roasted pumpkin, 159
  winter, pear soup with tarragon cream, 19
  winter, soup with sweet potato relish, 34
  winter vegetables & white bean ragout, 38
stock:
  chicken, 71
  corn, 106
  turkey, 71
  vegetable, 85
  vegetable, 152
strawberries, see berries

sugar-ginger glaze, 113
sweet potato:
  cakes, 16
  matchstick, 147
  pecan relish, 35
  winter, & confit of duck Napoleon with rapini, 16
  winter squash soup with, pecan relish, 34
tarragon:
  cream, 19
  creamy, dressing, 66
  roasted chicken with, peach sauce, 61
tomatillo, southwestern asparagus, corn &, soup, 69
tomato(es):
  arugula salad with raw sweet corn & sweet 100,
    102
  baked red snapper with, peppers & onions, 103
  chopped salad, 105
  concasse, 70
  creamed corn & marinated, with assorted basils,
    116
  grilled fish with heirloom, & salsa verde, 110
  Mediterranean pasta, 101
  petite aïoli: ahi tuna, potato & vegetable salad,
    154
  roasted, 39
  roasted salmon with oven-dried cherry, shiitake
    mushrooms & broccoli rabe, 114
  spicy tuna, caper, anchovy &, sandwiches, 104
  stuffed caramelized, with vanilla ice cream, 120
  summer Mediterranean gratin, 124
turnips:
  ragout of spring vegetables with aged sherry
    vinegar & green olive oil, 84
vinaigrette:
  citrus, 99
  Meyer lemon, 58
  Meyer lemon, 79
  simple, 169
  walnut, 31
  Zinfandel, 110
walnuts, see nuts
watercress:
  grilled asparagus with Meyer lemon vinaigrette
    & shaved Bellwether Pecorino Pepato, 58
  late summer salad: figs & melon with goat
    cheese & citrus vinaigrette, 99
zucchini:
  roasted gypsy pepper, ronde de nice squash
    & Toscano cheese bread pudding, 162
  summer Mediterranean gratin, 124
  winter vegetables & white bean ragout, 38